MESSAGES ON PRAYER

MESSAGES ON PRAYER

B. H. CARROLL

Founder and
First President of
Southwestern Baptist
Theological Seminary,
Fort Worth, Texas

Compiled by
J. W. Crowder

Edited by
J. B. Cranfill

BROADMAN PRESS | Nashville, Tennessee

© 1942 • Broadman Press

Nashville, Tennessee

422-07200

Library of Congress catalog card number: 42-23298

Printed in the United States of America

7.5JE6013

To

HARRISON CARROLL

of Los Angeles, California

*youngest son of B. H. Carroll, and one of the dearest and
most affectionate of all my friends, and in the hope
that as he journeys on in life he will assimi-
late more and more to the mental and
spiritual stature of his immortal
father, this book is most
lovingly dedicated by*

THE EDITOR

FOREWORD

PRAYER is the life line of Christianity. It is the alpha and omega of the Christian's earthly life. Christian activity, devotion, and achievement are all measured by the Christian's prayer life. The whole scheme of redemption is keyed to prayer. Jesus said: "Ask, and it shall be given you; knock, and it shall be opened unto you," and his invitation to wandering, burdened humanity was, "Come unto me, all ye that labour and are heavy laden, and I will give you rest."

> Prayer is the simplest form of speech
> That infant lips can try;
> Prayer the divinest strains that reach
> The Majesty on high.

From the agonies of the cross when he was dying, Jesus uttered this heartbreaking prayer: "Father, forgive them; for they know not what they do." None of us can ever forget the transfiguration scene, a description of which would bankrupt any vocabulary. We will not forget that from that sublime occasion these pungent and penetrating words emerged: "As he prayed, the fashion of his countenance was altered." The last words of dying Stephen yet reverberate through our wandering, sinning world: "Lord Jesus, receive my spirit!"

> Prayer is the Christian's vital breath,
> The Christian's native air,
> His watchword at the gates of death;
> He enters heaven with prayer.

In view of all these spiritual altitudes and immortalities, the reader will not wonder that my heart sings with inexpressible joy as I send out far afield this thirtieth volume of B. H. Carroll's great books I have been privileged to edit, publish, and cause to be published. It will soon be fifty-six years since

I published "The Agnostic," his great sermon against a quality of skepticism which was at the time oversweeping Waco and the surrounding country. Since that time there have appeared *Carroll's Interpretation of the English Bible,* a thirteen-volume set, and sermon books as follows: *Sermons, Baptists and Their Doctrines, Evangelistic Sermons, The River of Life, Inspiration of the Bible, Jesus the Christ, The Day of the Lord, Revival Messages, The Holy Spirit, Ambitious Dreams of Youth, The Faith That Saves, Christ and His Church, The Providence of God,* and *Christ's Marching Orders.*

As I have often said, in writing introductory words for these Carroll books, each one that appears seems to me the best one. The present volume is in this respect not unlike the others. One of the weakest links in the chain of Christian activities is found in our failure to sense the privileges and immortalities of prayer.

In her book, *The Fighting Angel,* Pearl Buck tells of her father, Dr. Absalom Sydenstricker, who was a Presbyterian missionary in China. When Pearl Buck was a child, she noted each morning, when her father would come in to breakfast, three red streaks on his forehead, but she was too timid to ask him what caused these streaks. When she grew older, she became sufficiently courageous to ask her father about these red streaks on his forehead. He then told her that before coming to breakfast each morning he spent an hour on his knees in prayer and the red streaks were the prints of his fingers on his forehead.

When my brother, Dr. T. E. Cranfill, now deceased, was practicing medicine in Waco, Texas, he was called to attend a dying Salvation Army captain. His recital of the last moments of this Christian worker was deeply impressive. This Salvation Army captain died with a light on his face never seen on land or sea. After his passing, my brother lingered to assist in laying him out. All the surroundings were indicative of the earthly poverty of this Christian man. My brother told me that when he saw this dead captain's knees, there were great callouses on both of them because of the fact that he had spent so much time in prayer.

In the present volume there are many great sermons, but perhaps the one that will to some be most impressive is the first one in the book with the title, "Accessibility of God Through Christ." That sermon has no counterpart in any sermonic literature that has come to my attention. The others are all noteworthy and inspiring. I commend to the reader all the sermons in this book, not only for reading but also for study.

It is proper to say that these sermons were compiled by Professor J. W. Crowder, A.B., D.D., of the Southwestern Baptist Theological Seminary, who was a long-time student of Dr. Carroll and who succeeded him in the chair of English Bible in the seminary. Professor Crowder has done great service in this enterprise, in which he and I have joined hands through the long years.

Loving acknowledgment is also registered here of the help on this and other Carroll books of my precious daughter, Miss Mabel Cranfill. On account of a long-time eye trouble, my reading ability has been greatly circumscribed. It is thus that my dear daughter has read to me every word in this book, and together we have served lovingly and gratefully in the preparation of this volume. It is not every scholar who can render the quality of service my daughter has rendered me. She not only has the journalistic gift, but also has had experience as my associate in other literary enterprises. She is a superb judge of literary values, is a good proofreader, and a delightful fellow worker, and I am therefore here acclaiming her and gratefully recording her invaluable help on this task.

I hope that each friend who reads this book will do another worthy deed by buying a copy of it to give to someone else who needs the help it brings. The book will help all of us who read it and it will help us more if we will aid in its wide circulation in our respective fields of service.

Dallas, Texas   J. B. CRANFILL

CONTENTS

I

ACCESSIBILITY OF GOD THROUGH CHRIST

TEXT: *O thou that hearest prayer, unto thee shall all flesh come.*—PSALM 65:2.

THE text asserts two propositions: (1) That God is a hearer of prayer, and (2) that he is ready to hear the prayers of all peoples, making it an obligation on all people to come to him in prayer.

Very early in that part of my life in which I began to be interested in the subject of religion came this difficulty: How can I get to God? As Job says: "Oh that I may know where I might find him! If I knew where I might find him I would come before him with my mouth filled with argument and as a man speaking face to face with a friend, I would state to him my case. But turning to the right hand I see his work, but him I cannot see. I feel that he is before me, but when I look there I do not see him. I realize that he is on my left hand and behind me and over me and under me, but when I turn about in any direction I don't know where to find him." This difficulty every heart experiences. That difficulty and a desire arising from it grew up together and kept growing among the children of men until it became a desire of all people that in some way God would make himself come-at-able, visible, approachable.

The promise was given in the Old Testament that the Desire of all nations should come, and when he came he would come to the Temple and come suddenly. Other Scriptures showed that when he came he would come as a revelation of the Father; that he would be himself the answer to the ten thousand questions of the human heart in the ten thousand varied experiences of human life, so that when we looked at him we would see as complete a representation of God, as complete a revelation of the state of God's mind toward men

[11]

as our fallible and finite nature would enable us to com-
prehend. He came to show the Father to us. So then when
we look at Christ, taking the record of his life that is given
to us in the Four Gospels, and studying it carefully with reference to this one point—Christ's approachableness—we then
get a true idea of God the Father's approachableness in
prayer.

The profoundest impression that has ever been made on
my life since I began to study the Bible was made on my
mind some ten days ago. I say none has ever come up to
that. It was past midnight and I was studying the subject.
I took the New Testament and read the Four Gospels through
at one sitting that night, noticing only one thing, to-wit: The
people who came to Christ and asked him for anything or
about anything, writing down on a piece of paper each case.
Where there was a great group at one time, I called that a
group case, but there are more than one hundred fifty
specific cases recorded. The great multitude were not num-
bered, but they were referred to in general terms. And when
reading the Four Gospels through with reference to that one
point only, of Christ's approachableness, I saw all flesh coming to him; I saw him giving an audience to all flesh, and
I contrasted in my mind earthly kings, earthly governors, as
to their come-at-ableness and approachableness.

If there were no other argument to prove to me the divinity
of Jesus Christ than this one, it is all-sufficient to establish
incontrovertibly that he is divine. It is a unique history—
"without a model and without a shadow." I do not believe
that all the kings and governors of the whole world, in a hundred years' time, give as many personal audiences to visitors
and applicants as Jesus Christ gave in the three years of his
public life. And nowhere else in history can there be found
an instance where there was absolute insistence upon this
point, that each case that came, whether man or devil, must
have individual and personal and continual access. More
than once the disciples sought to make themselves interme-

diaries between other people and Christ, and to become themselves the judges as to the kind of cases that should be presented, and in every instance they brought upon themselves stern and indignant rebuke, and the needy one seeking Christ found him for himself. Between that applicant and God there was nothing.

I say I never had such an impression made on my mind as that. I studied my own case. I thought that I was reasonably approachable, at least up to the average among men, and yet I know how it annoyed me if these applications were so continuous and persistent as to destroy my rest. Over and over again it is stated that in his case there was not time to eat, or rest; and in one instance we may infer from the record that his own mother and his brethren sought to take out a writ of lunacy against him because of this continual approachableness without regard to any personal comfort whatever.

If a devil wanted to say, "We know thee who thou art, thou Holy One of God, do not torment us before our time," he gave an answer. If the chief of the devils approached him and said, "I request that you let me sift your disciples," he heard him. If a woman came with a little babe in her arms and requested that he would put his hands upon that child and pray for it, and others would try to thrust her aside and tell her not to trouble the Master, he spoke out and said, "Suffer the children to come unto me, and forbid them not." If some selfish man, with his eye fixed wholly upon his own aggrandizement, wished Christ to cause a settlement of a contested inheritance, a purely secular matter, "Lord, make my brother divide the inheritance with me," he would allow himself to be approached. If a man in a dungeon, far away, and unable to come himself, his mind perplexed with doubt on account of being cut off from public and active life, sends messengers to inquire concerning this perplexity of his mind, without a word of censure he answers the question and sends back the reply.

So then, whether it was a demon or the chief of devils, whether it was a hating and malevolent Pharisee, or a Sadducee believing neither in God nor angels nor spirits, no matter who the being was, what the state of the being's mind, or the motive that prompted him to come, there was no sentinel stationed at the gate or at the door or in the palace that would deny the personal application. No red tape; no going through intermediate and subordinate officials. He stood as a revelation of God. "O thou that hearest prayer, unto thee shall all flesh come."

I say again that of all the impressions that have ever been made upon my mind from the study of God's Word, that is the deepest one I ever received and it continually abides with me. Its far-reaching signification takes hold of me by day and by night that Jesus Christ, as the revelation of the Father, as the express image of his person, coming to make known God to men, and on the matter of approachableness in every case of difficulty or distress, wrought, in the facts concerning his life, a demonstration of his divinity that is as immovable as a granite mountain, for there is no other such case in this world's history.

Now I make this point with you particularly, as I know there are some people here today deeply interested in the subject of religion. I do not care how old you are, nor how young; whether you are man or woman; whether you are good, bad, or indifferent. It does not make an atom of difference, the question or degree of your alienation from God. I do say that for yourself you can have instant and direct communication with God himself in settlement of your trouble, of your difficulty, and that all the preachers and all the churches on the earth are devoid of any authority to block your way, to impede your course; that you may yourself go to God and state your case.

That night I jotted down on paper the several points. As Jesus came to reveal God the Father, what revelation of God did he make on the social question, mixing with society?

What revelation of God was there in that?   And so I took down every case where Jesus Christ accepted an invitation to go to anybody's house, and I found that he never did reject an invitation, a respectful invitation, to take a meal with any family, and that his acceptance was in no case modified by the moral character of the one who invited him.   He received an invitation to a wedding.   He went.   He received an invitation to make his home in Simon Peter's house.   He accepted.   He was invited to stop with a little family in Bethany.   He accepted the invitation.   Three times over it is stated that Pharisees who disliked him, who hated him, invited him to come to their house for breakfast or dinner or supper, and every time he went—with this very suggestive and indeed startlingly revealing accompaniment—that he never went anywhere where his disciples would be forbidden to come.   He never went anywhere with the understanding that his presence in that house was to estop his teachings of the doctrine which he came to teach.   He never went to a house except either upon the express or implied understanding that while he was in that house, the door of approach to him by any lost soul in the world should be kept open, and some of the most remarkable cases of salvation are recorded of that kind, where he is the guest of the house of an enemy; where they are thinking evil of him, where he sits down and is kind and courteous and accepts the invitations, but yet silently the tide of those desirous of help pours in and comes right up to him, even when he is at the table eating, and while he eats, he hears and dispenses the blessings of life.

On one occasion his friends asked the privilege of giving him a supper complimentary to himself.   He accepted on the condition, as brought out in the history, that this same state of affairs should obtain, and so he was just as approachable there as he was at any other time.   This is a remarkable thing. I don't know anything like it in history.   Generally the idea is that as a man, if I go to a fashionable person's house, while I am in that fashionable person's house I must "do as Rome does." I must temporarily take upon myself the customs of that house. Isn't that true? Isn't it true that there are places where even preachers of the gospel either do not feel free to speak concerning Jesus Christ, or else do not care to speak concerning Jesus Christ? He was never in any such situation as that.

The next thing I marked down while studying the question was that a person who had recently been converted was very anxious that Jesus should come and meet a great many of his class. So he gave what you might call a sinners' dinner. Matthew was a publican. He had been a great sinner. Christ had saved him and he found Christ very precious to himself, and he said, "Lord, I want to give a dinner and I want to invite all the sinners you can meet to that dinner, and I want you to come. Will you come? Will you meet them?" When I got to that record where Matthew, the publican, gave this dinner to the publicans, and to Christ in contact with publicans, that they might see him to be the precious Saviour that Matthew had found him, I almost felt like shouting in view of the effect of it.

The next thing I noticed was this: That some of the people would say to Christ, "Depart! We do not want you!" and his treatment of cases of that kind. I found that his conduct varied here; that it varied according to the case, and now I will show you two examples to illustrate some cases. Wherever he came his purity was such, his manner was such, that sin felt itself discovered, unmasked, and his holiness was so impressive that if there was an evil heart in the crowd, that heart at once recognized the opposite and conflicting principle of holiness. Now on one occasion he stepped into a little boat and, by one or two incidents following each other, there came a revelation of his absolute spotlessness, of his holiness, a holiness that was awful. One man felt it and got down on his knees and said, "Lord, depart from me, for I am a sinful man." I noticed that when he was asked to depart in that way he did not depart. He considered that a good sign. He only pressed his company the more upon cases of that kind. But when the Gadarenes, who had been disturbed on account of the loss of the two thousand swine that, being filled with devils, cast themselves into the sea, when they came and implored him to depart, he went without a word. "If you ask me to go for that, I will go." "That is, I never force myself upon you when you want me to go in order that you may continue in iniquity without rebuke. If you say go, I will go."

I then noticed this: that while he never did refuse to see any poor man, any sick man, any sin-smitten man who desired to be saved, he did refuse to see the great who simply wanted to look at him from curiosity. Herod was king, and for three years he wanted to see Christ. He heard a great deal about him. He wanted an interview with this wonderful man. He never got the interview until just before Christ was crucified. Christ refused (peremptorily) voluntarily ever to permit himself to be seen by this man, but when he was arrested and brought before Herod, and Herod wanted him to work a miracle, just like you would ask a Japanese juggler to perform some dexterous feat of legerdemain, he answered not a word. The oracle was dumb.

I took a list of the cases of silence: "He answered not a word," and it brought out a curious contrast, that sometimes his silence was temporary, with a view to develop interest and test faith, as in the case of the Syrophoenician woman. She cried to him and "He answered not a word," but he was listening. She kept presenting her case and after a while he answered. But in the case of Pilate, in the case of Herod, in the case of Caiaphas, in all cases where there was an endeavor to force him to speak with a sinister end in view, or for the gratification of mere curiosity, he answered not a word. The oracle was dumb. As a sample, I will read you some applications that came to him. This one: "Lord, are they few that be saved?" Now this one, "Lord, when will the kingdom come?" Now he heard these people. He did not deny them access to his person. They presented those cases to him.

He declined to answer any of them. They were mere questions of curiosity. They had no moral significance in the world. The parties were not asking when the kingdom would come with a view to adjusting themselves to the kingdom. They were not asking if there were few that would be saved in order that if it was only a few they might endeavor more earnestly to be of the few. He knew what prompted them to make the request and he gave no straightforward answer to any of these, but he would say something like this: "You ask me if there be few that are saved. I say to you, Strive to enter in at the strait gate, for many shall seek to enter therein and shall not be able. I answer so far as the case touches you."

I then noted down every case where people came up to him and asked an explanation either of his kingdom or of a Scripture or of a parable. Now here are a lot of people coming for information. How do you treat these people? Are you approachable on that subject? There is a vast deal of ignorance in the world. The people want explanation of a great many things. Now what was the attitude of Christ toward seekers of information? I will state a case or two for you to think about.

One of them came to him by night early in his ministry. Nicodemus was very much disturbed about this kingdom of Jesus Christ. There is an honest inquiry, and oh, how honest the answer! Read that third chapter of John, where, though it was only one man, and that man came by night, and in Jesus' hours of rest, and presented his case and asked explanation upon it, what wonderful revelations of divine truth he gave! Then again, the disciples took him aside out of the crowd. He had been teaching in parables, and they took him aside and said, "Lord, expound unto us this parable." And how simple, and how lucid, and how like daylight is his explanation. The cases of that kind alone would be sufficient for a sermon.

I then considered this: How did Jesus stand with reference to family applications? His own family? Here are the cases that occurred: One when he was twelve years old, in the Temple; one at the marriage in Cana in Galilee; one when his mother and brothers wanted to stop his work because he was allowing his zeal to consume himself; one when his unbelieving brothers were goading him to go to Jerusalem and demonstrate his divinity by a miracle; and one when the woman cried out, "Blessed is the womb that bore thee." Now these are the cases where family considerations came in. How did he act on these cases? He placed himself, so far as the dispensation of the merits of his kingdom were concerned, absolutely beyond the pale of mere fleshly connection: "Wist ye not that I must be about my Father's business?" was the first answer. The second answer: "Woman, what have I to do with thee?" The third answer: "Who is my mother and who are my brethren? Whosoever doeth the will of God, the same is my father, my mother, my brother, my sister." To his unbelieving brothers this answer: "My time is not yet come; but your time is always ready." And the last was, "Instead of saying, Blessed is the womb that bore me, you had better say, Blessed is the one that doeth the will of God." I don't know of anything like that in history.

I then wrote down a list of all those cases where he was asked to use his religious influence in order to help out some selfish or secular thing. Hear some of the cases. That demoniac that he cured beyond the sea of Galilee had an intense desire to follow him and be with him. The record says he came down to the boat and wanted to get in, and pleaded to get in: "Lord, let me go with you." Jesus refused: "No, you stay here. You go home and tell your family what God has done for you. You become my preacher in this community. They are sending me away now. I am coming back. When I come back and find fruit from your work, that will be worth more to the cause of God than if you were simply allowed to get in this boat and follow me and be my companion. The one is more pleasant to you, but the other is duty." And whoever has studied that history in its chronological order will see that the next time that Christ came to that community (and once more he did come), thousands of people welcomed him, for it was there that he fed the five thousand men, besides women and children, there where he had prevented this restored demoniac from devoting his life selfishly and commanded him to devote it unselfishly.

I then marked these cases: He was at the house of that private family I told you about. There were three people in it, a brother and two sisters. One of the sisters was engaged in getting up what you might call a company dinner, or supper, I don't know which. The other was sitting at the feet of Jesus, to learn concerning his kingdom. Directly the one who was so much concerned in performing the household part of the matter, the hospitality part, came running in, very much vexed and worried, with this plea: "Lord, dost thou not care that my sister leaves all this burden on me?" Now would you think it lawful for you to carry a case of that kind to Jesus? Certainly you may. It makes no difference what the case is, you may take it to him; some little household matter, where you think that one member of the family is not doing his full part, but if you ever take it to Jesus, I would tell you not to be certain in your mind what is going to be his answer. He will let you state it, but when he answers you, he will answer you from no standpoint of selfishness, nor will he in his answer subordinate soul to body, nor will he subordinate religion to secular matters. He may say to you like he said to Martha, "Thou art cumbered with many cares," as if he had said, "You are taking a great deal of unnecessary trouble on yourself. Mary has chosen that better part. Yours is a good part if you don't allow your anxieties and fussings and fretfulness to carry you too far, but there is something better than that, Martha. There is something higher than that. It is a thousand times better for you to entertain Jesus in your heart for your soul's good, than it is that you should cook him a big supper or a big dinner and entertain him with merely temporal pleasures and comforts."

Then take this case I have referred to: "Lord, make my brother divide the inheritance." I could tell you some curious things but will not. A minister learns matters under confidence like a physician learns them; but I will state this fact: On one occasion I had a man to ask me to use my recognized influence as a preacher over a certain young man to induce him to marry the applicant's widowed daughter; and some cases worse than that. "I see religion is a power. I see it has an influence. I have an axe to grind. I have a political purpose to subserve. O religion, come help me out of this." The Lord Jesus Christ replied in a moment: "Man, who made me a judge over this matter?" And turning around to his disciples, he said, "Take heed that you beware of covetousness." This man comes to the Son of God and wishes him to use the spiritual power of the kingdom of God simply to better his financial condition.

I mention only one other case of this kind that I noted. A woman, and a Christian woman, one who had been exceedingly kind to him, had two very good boys, of whom she was very proud, and she had a right to be. I don't know any two boys of the time that would stand ahead of those two boys, and she knew that Jesus was very kind to both of them. Now the sacred history is about this: The boys, ashamed to ask for themselves, got their foolish mother to intercede. That is what the records show. They dared not look him in the face and say, "Lord, give us these privileges"—they did not dare to do it. But they stated their cases to their mother and got the mother to represent them. You remember the case. The mother of Zebedee's children came up to Jesus and said substantially, "Lord, give my son John the place on thy right hand in thy kingdom, and my son James the place on thy left hand in thy kingdom." Strange that they would ask that, if it had already been given to Peter, as some affirm, and stranger that he should say, "What you ask is not mine to give." And then he commenced to comment. "The lords of the Gentiles, the kings of the Gentiles, exercise lordship over them. Oh, let it not be so with you, not with you. Call no man master. One is your Master, even Christ, and you are brethren. When you talk about the primacy, who is the first? If any man would be first, if any man would be great in the kingdom of God, let him be your servant." O what other teacher taught like that!

Now I ask you to notice this point, for I am near the conclusion of all that I shall say this morning. I wrote down in parallel columns all the cases of this kind: the people who of themselves came to Christ, and the people who were brought to Christ by others, sometimes not interested themselves — the people that came, and the people that were brought. What about them? There was a difference in his treatment of these cases. Not that either one was rejected. For example, Bartimeus presents his own case, and that too when they were trying to keep him from getting to Jesus; when they were telling him to hush, he was troubling the Master, but he kept on presenting his own case: "O Jesus, thou son of David, have mercy on me." The answers of Christ in cases of that kind were overwhelmingly and instantly gracious.

But if a man was brought to him it was still gracious, but not so quick. Before he would be gracious, something had to be developed. Compare the instantaneous healing of Bartimeus who came, with this case: "And he cometh to Bethsaida, and they bring a blind man unto him, and besought him to touch him. And he took the blind man by the hand and led him out of the town; and when he had spat on his eyes and put his hands upon him, he asked him if he saw aught. And he looked up and said, I see men as trees, walking. After that he put his hands again upon his eyes, and made him look up; and he was restored, and saw every man clearly." This man was brought. See the effort to arrest his attention and excite a personal faith.

Now take the case of the deaf and dumb man. He did not manifest an atom of interest. Probably he was born deaf and dumb, and having those two channels cut off, his ideas were necessarily limited. They brought him. The record does not say that he did anything. Now mark that Jesus, in this case as in the case of the blind man cited, took that man off away from the crowd—took him by the hand, led him off. Now here the two stand alone. He is looking right in the eyes of this deaf mute, but how on earth can an idea be conveyed to him? Jesus puts his fingers to the deaf man's ears. Maybe that deaf man will infer from this action that something will be done to his ears for his hearing. Maybe he can be interested by touch and sign. He then reaches out and touches the man's tongue with his finger, as if by that sign to say, "I want to make that tongue speak. Are you getting interested? Are you taking hold?" Then without saying anything he lifted up his eyes to heaven and the man saw him. Now see how difficult to communicate an idea to a deaf and dumb man. Yet it must be done. This man was brought to Christ. Christ determined to help him, and by those three singular and yet appropriate methods, putting his fingers to his ears, touching his tongue, lifting up his eyes to heaven, and seeing that he had gotten his attention, he gazed right into his eyes and said, "Be opened," and the ear was opened and the tongue was loosed, and the man was healed.

I will close what I have to say today by referring to just one other class. Remember what the theme is, that Jesus Christ is to reveal the Father, that he is to reveal to you God's approachableness; that God is accessible, and that anybody may come to him; that he hears prayer, and that all flesh may come; that you may come for yourself; come sick or well, rich or poor, great or small, man or woman, human or devil, for yourself, you may come directly and state your case.

Now I wrote down on my piece of paper a class of cases that touched me so that I sat there in my chair and wept;

I could not help it. I don't know what happened to me. I felt, I suppose, somewhat like Paul felt when he said he didn't know whether he was in the body or out of it. I do know that to my mind the pictures of the scenes, all of them, passed before me as if I were an eyewitness. And what were they? The cases of silent appeal, where the situation was itself the petition, and no voice was heard and no written communication addressed to him, but just utter wretchedness, appealing to God's sight and compassion and mercy.

First, a case of despair. You remember the impotent man at the pool of Bethesda, who so long had been helpless, until at last despair had taken possession of him. There he lay without a hope, so helpless that he did not even turn his head when Christ came up; so hopeless he did not even ask for anything. But the case spoke for itself, and Jesus came up to him and asked him why he was in that condition. You have heard me tell about the Irish beggar. A rich English lord was driving through Ireland in his chariot and he passed the beggar on the roadside, who had evidently been sick for a long time—in rags, emaciated—and he expected that beggar to step out before the carriage and hold out his hat, but the beggar no more moved than a statue; he no more spoke than the sphinx, and his stillness and silence made the Englishman ask, "Why on earth don't you ask me to give you something?" With Irish eloquence the reply came, "Your honor, if me rags and me bones sticking out ask nothing, what more could me voice ask? O me rags and me bones make their silent appeal." So that case at Bethesda.

So of that woman whom Satan had bound for eighteen years. Nobody thought about her. Nobody interested himself in her behalf, and she never had a thought that anybody ever would. Bowed down until she looked like a beast going on all fours, hopelessly crippled, and Jesus saw it—the case spoke for itself. It was its own interpretation. The wretchedness and despair of it were a silent appeal to him, and he healed her.

Then the case of that widowed mother. Jesus and his
crowd were going up the hill to a city on top of the hill, and
just before his crowd got to the top of the hill, a funeral
procession came out of the town, coming down the hill, and
there was a mother who was a widow, and whose only son
was dead. She never said one word to Jesus. The case
spoke to the compassionate heart of the Son of God, and he
raised that boy to life. "Here, Mother, is your son!"

Take the case of Zaccheus. He had no more idea that
Jesus would condescend to speak to him than he had that an
angel from heaven would come down and stay all night in
his house, but he wanted to see him and he climbed up that
tree. The thought in that man's heart was: "I know I am
bad. I know I have been an extortioner. I know that I have
lived wrong in the sight of God, but I have heard about
Jesus and I want to see him. I do not suppose he will condescend to look at me; I have no idea that he will speak to
me, but I want to see him." But there in that tree, silently
looking at Jesus, the case spoke for itself, and Zaccheus was
startled when Jesus looked up and with a voice sweeter than
the chime of a marriage bell, said, "Zaccheus, come down. I
am going to your house today." O what a revolution in that
man! "Jesus speaks to me. Jesus is not ashamed to come
to my house. Jesus will come and stay with a wretched, miserable sinner, and without one word of upbraiding." And
salvation entered that house that day.

You know I cannot quote all the cases of approach to Jesus.
There are over one hundred fifty special instances, as I told
you, besides many groups, but I ask you to look at this one
picture. He had been teaching and healing all day, and when
it was sunset, great crowds came, bringing their sick and all
that had any disease and laid them down. The yard is full,
the streets are full, all out around the house, wherever you
look, here are sin and sorrow and suffering brought to Jesus
as to God. "O thou that hearest prayer, unto thee shall all
flesh come." And he goes around and with a touch and a

word and a look, healing and saving, until that city is filled with joy.

What unjust ideas I once had about God! What ideas I have now about God since I studied Jesus! I now know the Father; I know his approachableness. I know that he is not confined to Jerusalem, nor the mountains of Samaria, but everywhere on the face of the earth, a soul, any soul, no matter how sinful, may for itself come directly to Jesus and say, "God be merciful to me, a sinner," and salvation comes to that soul. Will you try it? I know that if any poor prodigal, homeless, helpless, ragged and wretched, will but arise and go to the Father, from afar off the Father will see him and run to meet him, and tenderly embrace him and kiss him much and welcome him with joy to light and home and melody and happiness.

Let no man dare to block the way to God. Let neither priest, apostle, nor devil forbid any petitioner direct access to God through Christ. Stand back, thou self-appointed peddler of the divine favors! Withdraw thy baneful shadow from the path of the comer to God! Come on, ye supplicants! Hear the Master: "Come unto me all ye that labour and are heavy laden, and I will give you rest." "Him that cometh to me I will in no wise cast out." Come on, mothers, with your babies! Come, blind Bartimeus! Come, thou prodigal! Come, Zaccheus and Matthew! Come, ye Magdalenes! Come, dying thieves! The door is wide open by day and night. No sentinel blocks the way. No disciple may forbid. Come your-self to God himself. O sinner, dying sinner, do come!

II

TWENTY PRAYERS OF JESUS

PART I

TEXT: *We know not what we should pray for as we ought . . . Lord, teach us to pray.*—ROMANS 8:26; LUKE 11:1.

OUR most lamentable ignorance is in regard to prayer. "We know not what we should pray for as we ought." No difficulty in human life is more common than perplexity arising from this ignorance. We are taught that our Heavenly Father has established a throne of grace, to which we are invited to come boldly and obtain help in every time of need, but we do not seem to know how to come. Any reliable information on this subject would be of vast practical value to Christian people. A part of our text says, "Lord, teach us to pray," showing that prayer is something to be learned, and that the teacher is Christ.

It is purposed, therefore, today to ask you to become disciples of Christ with reference to prayer. There are three ways set forth in the Scriptures by which we may learn of Christ concerning prayer: (1) We may thoughtfully observe the prayers offered by Christ, in order to learn the proper matter and manner of praying. (2) We may study from the fourfold history of Christ his reception of the petitions offered to him, and learn from the character of the petitions accepted or rejected what petitions ought to be addressed to God. (3) We may study all of the lessons on prayer given by Christ. We have thus marked out for our consideration three methods of learning from Christ about prayer: the kind of prayers that Christ offered, the kind of prayers Christ favorably heard, and his instructions concerning prayer.

To understand this subject thoroughly it will be necessary to go through the Four Gospels on each division, tracing each line of thought from its inception in the gospel history to its consummation, and by the use of a harmony, studying each lesson in its proper chronological order. It will thereby be demonstrated in this, as in all other departments of truth taught by Christ, that there is both a development and a system. Our sermon today will be confined to the first part of this general theme, that is, the prayers Christ offered. I have read all of the Four Gospels through in the last two days in order to note and classify the occasion, the subject matter, and the manner of Christ's praying. It is my purpose to call your attention to twenty of these prayers in their consecutive order. Others may have escaped notice, but I know that these twenty are there.

First, Jesus prayed for the Holy Spirit before beginning to teach. The history is given in the following Scriptures: "Now it came to pass, when all the people were baptized, that, Jesus also having been baptized, and praying, the heaven was opened, and the Holy Spirit descended in a bodily form, as a dove, upon him, and a voice out of heaven, Thou art my beloved Son; in thee I am well pleased. And Jesus himself, when he began to teach, was about thirty years of age" (Luke 3:21-23 ASV).

In his first letter to Timothy, Paul declares the church to be the pillar and ground of the truth, and among the elements of the truth which the church is to teach is this, "God was justified in the Spirit." The passage from Luke is at least a partial history of Jesus' justification in the Spirit. It seems that when he became God in the flesh, the Holy Spirit bore witness to his divinity though veiled in the flesh. The coming of the Spirit upon him at his baptism is referred to thus: "Him hath God the Father sealed," and again, "He was anointed

with the Holy Ghost and with power." Yet again, he himself
refers to it thus:

> The Spirit of the Lord is upon me,
> Because he anointed me to preach good tidings to the poor:
> He hath sent me to proclaim release to the captives,
> And recovering of sight to the blind,
> To set at liberty them that are bruised,
> To proclaim the acceptable year of the Lord.

From these scriptural testimonies it is evident that the
object of the coming of the Spirit upon him was to accredit
him as a divine messenger and to glorify him for his work.
We see at once then the appropriateness of the prayer that
he offered. He was made known to Israel by his baptism,
as the Messiah. His baptism introduced him openly to his
public work. Feeling the magnitude of the work committed
to him, as he was coming up out of the water, he prayed for
the Holy Spirit, and the answer was instantly granted. The
question naturally arises, of what practical value is this lesson
to us? Seeing Jesus praying, and praying for the Spirit just
after his baptism, just before he enters upon his public ministry, what does it suggest to us? Evidently that if our Lord
himself would not teach until anointed, endued and filled by
the Spirit, it would be a great presumption in us to attempt
religious teaching without enduement of power. Our first need
as Christians is to be accredited to the world and to be qualified for our duties toward the world. We know, therefore,
one object of prayer is to pray for the Holy Spirit.

Though he had instructed his disciples through more than
three eventful years, and though he had given them a commission to go and preach the gospel to every creature, he yet
said to them, "Tarry ye in Jerusalem. Wait until you are
endued with power from on high." They needed to be accredited. They needed to be qualified for their work, and hence
we learn that during the days that they waited, they assembled
in an upper chamber in Jerusalem, the men and the women,

and prayed for the Holy Spirit, whose outpouring upon them is so vividly set forth in the second chapter of the Acts.

Do you at the present time need the Holy Spirit? As a Christian do you feel powerless to discharge the obligations resting on you? Do you feel conscious that it is impossible for you in your own strength to do what God requires you to do? Will you be so presumptuous as to attempt these solemn and holy duties before you are endued with power from on high? How can you preach the gospel except with the Holy Spirit sent down from heaven? How can you even pray, since we are told in the very first part of our context that it is the Spirit that helpeth our infirmities with groanings unutterable? Do you need encouragement to pray for the Holy Spirit? Hear then the words of our Lord: "And I say unto you, Ask, and it shall be given you; seek, and ye shall find; knock and it shall be opened unto you. For everyone that asketh receiveth; and he that seeketh findeth; and to him that knocketh it shall be opened. And of which of you that is a father shall his son ask a loaf and he give him a stone? or a fish, and he, for a fish, give him a serpent? Or if he shall ask an egg, will he give him a scorpion? If ye, then, being evil, know how to give good gifts unto your children, how much more shall your Heavenly Father give the Holy Spirit unto them that ask him?"

If then, the first prayer offered by our Saviour was for the Holy Spirit to qualify him for his work, and if the apostles prayed for and received the Holy Spirit before they entered upon their great work, and if you are encouraged by the last Scripture read to pray for the Holy Spirit, we may rest assured that this is one thing for which it is always proper to pray, and we also learn the manner in which we should ask —that we should ask as a child in need addresses a parent, and with the same expectation of immediately receiving what we ask for.

Second, he prayed against the selfish spirit of monopoly. Following the order of Broadus' *Harmony* we have the following history of the case: "And in the morning, a great while before day, he rose up and went out, and departed into a desert place, and there prayed. And Simon and they that were with him followed after him; and they found him, and say unto him, All are seeking thee. And he saith unto them, Let us go elsewhere unto the next towns that I may preach there also; for to this end came I forth" (Mark 1:35-38). Luke adds: "The multitude sought after him, and came unto him, and would have stayed him, that he should not go from them. But he said unto them, I must preach the good tidings of the kingdom of God to the other cities also" (Luke 4:42-43).

He had but fairly commenced his great ministry in Galilee. Capernaum as his home was the special recipient of his benefits. In the synagogue there he had cast out an unclean spirit, causing the people to cry out in amazement, "What is this? A teaching with authority! He commandeth even the unclean spirits and they obey him." The record then states that the rumor went forth concerning him unto every place roundabout. Then follows the healing of Peter's mother-in-law, and then at sundown the bringing together of vast numbers of sick people and demoniacs, and his healing them all. He read their hearts. He recognized their desire to pre-empt his great services. They had no thought of others.

Now, under these conditions, when all the multitude were seeking him and desirous of retaining him in their place, selfishly concerned about their locality alone, as if it were lawful to monopolize salvation, he, a great while before day, goes out to a desert place and prays. Such inordinate selfishness was not friendly to the spiritual lessons that he wished to impart to the people. It shut their eyes to the second great commandment: "Thou shalt love thy neighbour as thyself," and narrowed and depreciated his mission. To localize Christ and his gospel denies that the other parts of the world have need of him; hence this prayer.

Now what is the solemn lesson to us? What objects of prayer does it suggest? Finds it nothing in our hearts to rebuke? Do you sit there prayerless, brother, saying within your heart: "I would pray, but I know not what to pray for?" Pray for this, then: "Lord, preserve my heart from selfishness—let me not narrow my concern to Waco, or Texas, or the United States. Lord, make me see the destitution in other cities. Open my ear to hear every Macedonian cry, Come over and help us! Help me to realize the unity of the race and the universality of thy mission of redemption. Lord, help me to feel that Paradise is roomy and in my Father's house are many mansions; that it will not crowd and jostle me if from every tribe and tongue and kindred the blood-washed may come."

Third, he prayed against the spirit of carnal excitement that magnified the temporal benefits of miracles above the spiritual lessons of his kingdom. Leaving Capernaum he had preached and healed in other cities of Galilee until the excitement was irrepressible. It culminates at the cleansing of the leper, whom he had charged to tell no man, and who had yet the more published abroad what had been done. The result was that Jesus could no more openly enter the city. There was no more an opportunity for teaching. The claim for the body and its wants crowded out the soul and its wants. So we learn from Luke 5:16: "But he withdrew himself in the desert and prayed."

Again the question arises: What practical lessons are here to be learned for us? Evidently that when our ministry generates an excitement not friendly to the teaching of the kingdom of God, an excitement more carnal than spiritual, and if it can neither be avoided, nor allayed, we are constrained by the example of Christ to turn away and betake ourselves to prayer. He is wise who can keep a reformation within due bounds; who can prevent a movement inaugurated by himself from getting ahead of him and dragging him where he would not go; who can repress the lawless and irresponsible elements that flock to any new movement that has power to attract attention. Hence we may always pray: "Lord, help us to build surely, even if we must build slowly. Help us to keep the soul on top. And give us wisdom to see when carnal elements are predominating, and grace to withdraw from a publicity that means evil and not good."

Fourth, he prays before ordaining preachers. Our record says, "And it came to pass in these days that he went out into the mountain to pray, and he continued all night in prayer to God. And when it was day he called his disciples; and he chose from them twelve whom he also named apostles." This case speaks for itself. It tells its own story, and evidently sets forth its appropriate lesson, that putting men into the ministry was no slight thing in the estimation of Christ; that the work of the ministry was the most important thing committed to man; that the office of the ministry is the highest known in time, and that when men are to be inducted into this holy and responsible office, there should be intense and long continued prayer to God that they may be qualified for their duties and faithful in the discharge of them; that they may study to show themselves worthy workmen, rightly dividing the Word of God.

And if the Lord, even after instructing for a long time those whom he had called to be his disciples, would not set them apart formally to the work of the ministry without spending a whole night in prayer, do we not sin against the example when we lay hands suddenly on men and induct novices into this high and responsible work? Certainly we may learn here that one of the objects for which Christians may pray is that the teachers of religion may not lightly take upon themselves this work, and may faithfully address themselves to its performance.

It is said that there are a thousand Baptist preachers in Texas, regularly ordained, who are neither pastors of churches, nor missionaries, nor teachers in schools—men without any charge. Was God mistaken in calling these men to preach, or were the churches mistaken in putting them into the ministry with undue haste? Doesn't such a lamentable fact as

this vast horde of unemployed men call upon us not only to
exercise more caution in the matter of ordination, but to
offer devout, earnest, and long continued prayer to God that
we may make no mistake? Is it possible that some of these
men failed to find employment because not apt to teach
others, or because, though apt, they would not study to show
themselves approved unto God; others because, having put
their hands to the plow, they look backward, and others because they are not willing to endure hardness as good soldiers
of Jesus Christ?

And if there be any of these possibilities, does it not indicate that sin lieth at the door of the churches, which without
due consideration, and especially without importunate
prayer, laid hands on men who were not called of God, nor
sent? Ah, me! What a question is this ministerial question!
Brother, if ever you find yourself out of objects of prayer
known to be lawful, concentrate your devotion on this point:
Pray for preachers! Pray for wiser churches! Is it possible
that some churches grind out a lot of preachers as some
colleges were once wont to make D.D.'s?

Fifth, he prayed that men might see the spiritual nature of
his kingdom. By combining the record of Matthew (14:22),
Mark (6:45), and John (6:15) we learn that after the feed-
ing of the five thousand men, besides the women and children,
from the five loaves and two little fishes, a tremendous excitement was engendered in the minds of the people. This
excitement was shared by the apostles themselves. The direction of the excitement was this: To play the part of Rome's
Pretorian Guard. Jesus, perceiving that they were about to
come and take him by force to make him a king, first compelled the disciples to take shipping and go to the other side
of the Sea of Galilee. They very reluctantly obeyed him. He
then very abruptly dismissed the multitude and himself went
up into the mountain apart to pray. The time is night. As
it is near the Passover, the moon is full. The grassy lawn
on the eastern mountain slopes of the Sea of Galilee, that had

lately been populous with the thousands of people ready to be fed by miraculous intervention, is now silent in the moonlight. High up on the mountain, all alone, Jesus is praying. Far below him on the Sea of Galilee his disciples are distressed, not only on account of his absence, but because of the storm that prevents them from reaching their destination. He sees them and he is praying.

Yet many other times will he have to resist this popular impulse to make him a king, whose throne was to be in Jerusalem, whose reign would be temporal, whose miraculous power would be exercised in delivering the people from the dominion of the Romans, and in obtaining the sovereignty of the world. But it was not for this he came. His kingdom was not of this world, and when he saw that this feeling had gotten to a point where it could be no longer controlled and that it was largely shared by the disciples themselves, he dismisses the people and sends the disciples away, that he may pray to God that they may have a proper conception of his mission and work. The history of this case is to be found in the fourteenth chapter of Matthew, sixth of Mark and the sixth of John.

What does the lesson suggest to us? While we may not share the gross ideas of the kingdom of the Messiah that caused the Jews of his time to misapprehend the nature of his work, yet is it not true that to a less degree at least we lose sight of the fact that the kingdom of God is not of this world—that it is spiritual in its nature—that the weapons of our warfare are not carnal—that the kingdom of heaven does not come by observation? It is neither "lo here" nor "lo there." It is within us. It consists not of meat and drink, but of righteousness and joy and peace in the Holy Ghost. Do not many of our churches, especially in the great cities, forget in the magnificence of their building, in the richness of their furniture, in the costly pealing organ, in the stained windows and softened light, in the rented pews and hired choirs, in the philosophical essays which have taken the place of the pulpit exposition of God's Word—do not these need to pray for a clearer and more spiritual understanding of his kingdom and mission here upon the earth?

It is not enough to condemn the faults of past ages. We should address ourselves to the correction of our own faults, and each one here today ought to be asked, My brother, my sister, is there not even with you some fault in the sight of God with reference to the spirituality of the reign of Christ upon the earth? What is the trend of your thought, of your life, of your religious service? Is it formal, ritualistic, consisting in mere rites and ceremonies? Is it heartless, external? Is it rationalistic, "liberal," according to modern phraseology? Does it subordinate the religious to the political, as did the Herodians of the time of Christ? Oh, is it not necessary to ask ourselves if we do not need Christ's caution: "Take heed and beware of the leaven of the Pharisees, and the leaven of the Sadducees, and the leaven of the Herodians"?

Sixth, he prayed that his immediate disciples, at least, might have a God-revealed spiritual faith in him as the Messiah. Our record says, "And it came to pass that as he was praying alone, the disciples were with him, and he asked them saying, Who do the multitudes say that I am?" (Luke 9:18.) We are not told in words for what Jesus was praying on this occasion, but it is easy to infer the object of his prayer from the context. The great Galilean ministry was ended; miracle and parable and precept had fulfilled their mission. Never again as a teacher was Jesus to labor among these people around the Sea of Galilee. Privately afterward, it is true, he passed through the section of country on his way to Jerusalem, and incidentally there might be some manifestation of his power, but his great ministry was ended, and ended forever, so far as that section was concerned. He had now, at the close of his work, retired from the jurisdiction of Herod in Galilee, and approaching Caesarea Philippi, he is about to sum up the results of his great Galilean work. He is quite certain that men, the mixed multitude, have various opinions concerning him and his mission. Some think him only a man, but a good man; some think him an impostor; some think him John the Baptist; some, Elijah, some Jeremiah. Why, then, is he praying? Evidently he is praying that his immediate disciples may have a God-revealed faith in his Messiahship and in his divinity.

We gather this because, as soon as the prayer was over, he began to catechize the disciples, drawing out from them who, having mixed with the multitude, were cognizant of popular thought, the opinions entertained concerning him, and following it up with the emphatic question, "Who say YE that I am?" And when Peter answered for the rest, as well as for himself, and impulsively cried out, "Thou art the Christ, the Son of the living God," the heart of Jesus glowed with happiness. His prayer was answered and in his exultation he said, "Blessed art thou, Simon Barjona; flesh and blood hath not revealed it to thee, but my Father who is in heaven." It seems then that Peter's confession exhibited faith—that it bears the relation to Christ's prayer that effect does to cause. It is easy, then, for us to draw from this example of Christ's praying a practical lesson profitable to us.

There would be no need for prayer if faith were a mere intellectual perception of the truth of a proposition—if it were head-faith only, if it came from flesh and blood, or from the will of man. But, as no man can come to Christ except by faith, and as none can come except the Father draw him, those who do receive him, even believing on his name, are born not of flesh nor of blood nor of the will of man, but of God. Paul in preaching relied not on the words of man's wisdom, but only on the demonstration of the Spirit, because he would not have man's faith to stand in man, but in God.

Then here is an object of prayer that we need never misunderstand, no matter who is preaching, no matter how apt to teach, how eloquent in speech, how accomplished in literary acquirements, how fervent in animal spirits, the faith of the gospel, the true faith which makes a man a Christian, must

be a God-revealed faith; hence, we need to pray in connection
with all teaching, with all preaching, that God himself would
give faith to the hearer. And it is on this account that Paul
said, "What is Paul and what is Apollos? Servants by whom
ye believed even as God gave to every man." That is why
we should pray for sinners. That is why preaching, however
clear its conceptions, however forcible and cogent its argument, is ineffective without the intervention of God.

So, then, if you are concerned upon the subject of not
knowing what to pray for as you ought, do look at this lesson.
Our Saviour himself holds it up for our admonition. It is
lawful, it is enjoined, it is urgently needed that we should
pray that men might have God-given faith. The text shows
that Peter's faith apprehended three things: 1. That Jesus
was the Messiah, that is, anointed to be the prophet, priest
and king. It recognizes his office. 2. It apprehended his
divinity: "Thou art the Son of God." 3. It apprehended
his filial connection with the living God, and not a dead
heathen deity. But this was far from being the highest development of faith. This much must be clear in order to the
next, and what next? He wanted to teach them that he
was to be a suffering Messiah, the necessity of his vicarious
atonement, praying that they might see him as the Messiah,
and as divine, and that prayer being answered, it laid the
foundation for the next teaching, and so we learn that from
that time—that is, from the time of the confession of this
faith, he began to show them plainly that he must go to
Jerusalem, to be rejected of the Sanhedrin, and to suffer and
die for his people.

Seventh, he prayed that his people may see glimpses of his
glory, lest they should be depressed by views of his humiliation. The record says, "And it came to pass about eight
days after these sayings, he took with him Peter and John and
James, and went up into the mountain to pray. And as he
was praying the fashion of his countenance was altered and
his raiment became white and dazzling. And behold, there

talked with him two men, which were Moses and Elijah, who appeared in glory and spoke of his decease which he was about to accomplish at Jerusalem."

From this record it is evident that this is the reverse side, the bright side of the dark view just before presented of his rejection and passion. Seeing from Peter's rebuke how little his faith in his Messiahship and divinity was ready even now to recognize his vicarious atonement, and realizing the depression of spirit that with their views of him would necessarily follow the announcement of his speedy death, we may understand at a glance the object of the prayer here recorded. Evidently he prayed that this very Peter, and others with him, to whom the idea of his passion was abhorrent, should see the glory that was to follow that passion, shortly to take place at Jerusalem. Hence we call this the prayer for transfiguration. The prayer that, in miniature, might be seen the majesty and glory of the second coming of Christ.

Surely if arising from this death at Jerusalem there should come a change of glorifying his face, that would make his garments white and glistening; that would introduce him unto majesty and glory; that would prefigure their own redemption from sorrow and death, it would go far toward reconciling their minds to what before had been so abhorrent. While the disciples seem not to have gathered the lesson which was intended at the time, yet we learn from Peter's later testimony that it was not altogether lost on him. That testimony is: "For we did not follow cunningly devised fables when we made known unto you the power and coming of our Lord Jesus Christ, but were eyewitnesses of his majesty. For he received from God the Father honor and glory, when there came such a voice to him from the excellent glory, 'This is my beloved Son in whom I am well pleased'; and this voice we ourselves heard out of heaven when we were on the holy mount."

As Moses and Elijah were present in this transfiguration scene, one who had died and the other who had been trans-

lated, one representing the law and the other the prophets and
both speaking with him of his decease which he was about
to accomplish at Jerusalem, there must have been a momen-
tous connection between that death and the translation of
Elijah and the hope of Moses; and so with all of the classes
represented by these two men. It represented the power and
the majesty of his second coming, in this: at his second coming, the dead will be raised; Moses who died was there; at
his second coming the living Christians will be translated
without death; Elijah who was translated was there. So, on
a simple and representative miniature scale, there was given
in the transfiguration scene two of the mightiest events which
attend Christ's second coming—the resurrection of the dead
and the translation of the living, both resurrection and
translation arising from the meritorious ground of his vicarious death, which Peter seemed so much to deprecate. Hence
we call this the reverse side, the bright side of the other picture presented, the one which showed in sorrowful colors his
humiliation and his passion.

Again the question arises: If Christ prayed that his disciples might be guarded against depressions arising from his
pre-announced death by a revelation of the glory to follow,
what lawful object of prayer does it suggest to us? There
are parts of the path of our earthly pilgrimage full of thorns
and leading up steep declivities; parts of the way are overshadowed by clouds reaching down into the very valley of the
shadow of death. Sometimes we are called upon to bear things
that are almost unbearable, and to do things, in the weakness
of the flesh, almost impossible; sometimes we sorely hunger
for the viands of the heavenly banquet, and crave with intense
longing the joys of everlasting and final deliverance.

In such a time, is it not well to pray that our heavenly
Father take us for a while to the top of some high mountain,
from whose summit, through the clear atmosphere of that lofty
altitude, we may see the Heavenly City itself, and, though
from afar, may catch the glittering sheen of the apparel of its

inhabitants and anticipate something of the gladness that wells up from the hearts of the finally redeemed?

Through the Holy Spirit is given unto us a pledge, an earnest, a forecast of what God will ultimately bestow on us. As the grapes of Eschol, borne far away from their parent stem, as a sample, enabled the Israelites in the desert to judge of the fertility and fruitfulness of the goodly land which God had given them, so these partial glimpses, these transfiguration scenes here on earth, enable us, because of what they forecast in future happiness, to take up again the burden of life and bear it manfully and bravely for the few days remaining.

Thus Paul, whether in the body or out of the body, he could not tell, was caught up to the third heaven, into the Paradise of God, and saw things unlawful to utter. And thus in part, at least, what the eye hath not seen, what the ear hath not heard nor the heart conceived of, the things which God hath in reservation for them that love him, the Holy Spirit, in answer to prayer, reveals to us here and now. It is only intended for a temporary support of the weary and desponding soul which, from hope deferred, had been made sick by delay. So then, brother, sister, when your burden becomes too heavy, when life's ways become too dark, when the heart is too sore, when you are ready to perish, it is not amiss to pray to God to open the heavens, and through a rift in the sky to shine down into your heart some of the light of the Glory World.

Eighth, a prayer of thanksgiving for the success of his ministers. The record says: "And the seventy returned with joy, saying, Lord, even the devils are subject to us in thy name. And he said unto them, I beheld Satan fall as lightning from heaven. Behold I have given you authority to tread upon serpents and scorpions, and tread on all the powers of the enemy; and nothing shall in any wise hurt you. Howbeit, in this rejoice not, that the spirits are subject unto you; but rejoice that your names are written in heaven. In

that same hour he rejoiced in the Holy Spirit, and said, I
thank thee, O Father, Lord of heaven and earth, that thou
didst hide these things from the wise and didst reveal them
unto babes; yea, Father; for so it was well pleasing in thy
sight."

We have considered one prayer of Christ, offered just before the twelve apostles were sent out to work in Galilee.
That was a prayer in deep and intense anxiety that they
might faithfully fulfil their mission. Here is a prayer of
thanksgiving. The occasion is not the outgoing, but the home-
coming of the seventy sent out to work in Judea. Jesus rejoices
in spirit. He thanks the Father, Lord of heaven and earth.

This teaches us a very solemn lesson. Men, weak in themselves, men having but little in an external, or intellectual, or
educational way, were yet qualified to turn the world upside
down. They had gone forth in his name, had cast out devils,
had trodden serpents and scorpions under their feet, had exercised power over the evil one; wherever they went the strongholds of the enemy had fallen before them. Jesus, in spirit
and from afar, had watched the progress of their missionary
labor.

He says, "I beheld Satan fall as lightning from heaven."
That is, the lightning from heaven suddenly falls to the
ground, so Jesus had seen Satan fall before the onslaught of
these seventy untutored men who went forth in the power of
the Spirit of God. They were the babes; they could not be
classed with the wise and the understanding; and Jesus rejoiced that through such weak and humble instrumentalities
the revelation of God was made to men.

Well might he rejoice at it. Well might he offer a prayer of
thanksgiving, that Satan and his demons and their strongholds
fell before these humble ministers of the gospel, for if only
the great men of the world, if only the wise men, if only
the mighty scholars were able to overthrow Satan and lead
souls to Christ, how little of the empire of Satan would ever
be vanquished, since so few of this class, kept back by intel-

lectual pride, kept back by their love for glory, think it a mission lofty enough for them, to be humble heralds of the cross. Therefore it had been well pleasing to God to choose the weak things of this world in the accomplishment of his designs. Gathered in the museum of religious collections, we see very little heavy armament capable of sending projectiles through the strongest armor plate, or of beating down the thickest wall. We see few fine tempered Damascus blades, but we see the sling of David, Gideon's pitchers and lamps, Shamgar's ox goad, the jaw bone of an ass in the hand of Samson, and such like things, blessed of God to the pulling down of the strongholds of Satan and of the world. It teaches us every one to pray with rejoicing when we see the powers of Satan falling under the triumphs of the gospel, and that we ought to thank God for every such humble, successful minister of grace.

And for myself, I hesitate not to say that I would go a greater distance and at a greater cost to shake the hand of some untutored man, some man of poverty, some man of scanty resources, who yet by simple faith in God, relying alone upon the demonstration of the Spirit and power, had preached with the Holy Ghost sent down from heaven, making the gospel the power of God unto the salvation of lost souls, than nearer home to shake the hand of one who carried a dozen titles, gifted in natural endowments, cultured and accomplished in his attainments, yet who failed practically in leading souls to Christ, whose intellectual and educational powers seemed to serve no other purpose in the pulpit than to put the bread of life above the reach of the people and to lull drowsy souls to sleep while he eloquently and learnedly discussed philosophy and metaphysics and liberalism and rationalism and higher criticism.

I repeat the words of Dr. Broadus: "Let us bear in mind that the early progress of Christianity, that great and wonderful. progress to which we still appeal as one of the proofs of its divine origin, was due mainly to the labors of obscure men, who have left no sermons, and not even a name to history, but whose work remains plain before the All-seeing Eye, and whose reward is sure. Hail, ye unknown, forgotten brethren! We celebrate the names of your leaders, but we will not forget that you fought the battles and gained the victories. The Christian world feels your impress, though it has lost your names. And not only are these early laborers not unknown, but most of them were in their own day little cared for by the great and learned. Most of them were uneducated. . . . Not only in the first centuries there were these uncultivated but good and useful men, but such preachers have abounded from that day to this, in every period, country, and persuasion in which Christianity was making any real and rapid progress."—*History of Preaching*, pp. 49-51. And if we are like Jesus, we will rejoice in their triumphs over Satan and thank God that the work of salvation was committed to them instead of to the wise and noble and great of this world.

Ninth, he prayed that his disciples might desire to learn to pray. Our record says: "And it came to pass as he was praying in a certain place that when he ceased, one of his disciples said unto him, Lord, teach us to pray" (Luke 11:1). Again we are left to infer the object for which Jesus prayed. We gather that object from what followed the prayer. There was something in the manner of his praying, its solemnity, its reverent spirit, that made an awful impression upon the minds of the disciples, leading them not only to see that they did not know how to pray, but provoking a desire to learn, and inducing them to ask him to teach them and to lead them into a docile attitude on the subject, receiving instruction as to the manner and matter of praying.

Only recently I was much impressed by a communication from Dr. Robertson of the Theological Seminary at Louisville, published in the "Religious Herald," upon the irreverent manner of modern prayer. He states the case of one who paused at the entrance of a church, not knowing whether it would be right to create a disturbance by going in just at that time, for from some signs he supposed that they were engaged in prayer. But he hesitated because he saw very many others that did not seem to be engaged in prayer. While the voice of the pleader seemed to be the voice of prayer, while the kneeling attitude of one or two seemed to suggest prayer, while the partially bowed heads of one or two others seemed to somewhat indicate prayer, yet the most of the people were sitting up, looking around, some of them whispering, some laughing; so there was made upon his mind the impression that many of that congregation were guilty of profanation.

Is this praying? Did Jesus so pray? Oh, if that thoughtless, irreverent crowd could have seen him pray one time, marked his reverent tone in using the name of God, the reverent uplifting of his eyes to heaven—if they could have heard one time the gracious words that fell from his lips, would not the impression have been made on them that they didn't know how to pray? Would they not now from the memory of it be compelled to lay aside their unseemly manner in the midst of public devotion and cry out in agony, "Lord, teach us to pray"?

There is one member in my congregation whose presence always cheers me, and whose absence always depresses me. It is because of his reverent manner in the house of God. None ever knew him to stop at the door and enter into idle conversation with those loitering there; none ever knew him, after taking his seat, to read letters or newspapers, or to engage in any sort of word or action that would attract to himself public attention, but evidently drawing in every wandering thought, and evidently fixing his mind on the occasion of the gathering, endeavoring to prepare himself by devout meditation for the duties of the hour. It is always an encouragement for a preacher to see his face.

It should teach us, it seems, that our devotions, the elements of our devotions, are always calculated to make an impression for good or evil on the unconverted. God is not the

author of confusion. All of our services should be unto edi-
fication. They should never be so conducted as to leave upon
the mind of the unlearned or of the unbelievers the impression
that we are hypocrites.

Paul says, "Wherefore tongues are for a sign, not to them
that believe, but to the unbelieving; but prophesying is for a
sign, not to the unbelieving but to them that believe. If
therefore the whole church is assembled together and all
speak with tongues, and there come in men unlearned or
unbelieving, will they not say that ye are mad? But if all
prophesy and there come in one unbelieving or unlearned, he
is reproved by all, he is judged by all; the secrets of his heart
are made manifest; and so he will fall down on his face and
worship God, declaring that God is among you indeed."

"Lord, teach us to pray." Lord, teach us to sing; Lord,
teach us to preach; Lord, teach us to teach; so that the
stranger as he enters the door will say, "Truly God is among
these people"; so that the sinner may be convinced in his
heart of his sins by the very earnestness of God's people.

The rest of the subject must be deferred to the night dis-
cussion, but before I dismiss you, brethren, I would ask you
to fix in your mind these several occasions of Christ's praying, and the stated or inferred objects for which he prayed,
that we may learn from them how and for what we should go
to the throne of grace in order to obtain the divine favor.
"Prayer is the Christian's vital breath, the Christian's native
air." The spirit of prayer then is the measure of our religion. It is not the cry of superstition; it is not the muttering
of ignorance; it is not the mechanical and perfunctory lip
service of the formalist or of the ritualist. It should come from
the heart; it is God-inspired. It goes to God. And from
these lessons of our Lord Jesus Christ, and those to be presented tonight, let us see if we cannot say to ourselves, we have
learned somewhat how to pray and what things to pray for.

III

TWENTY PRAYERS OF JESUS

PART II

TEXT: *We know not what we should pray for as we ought. . . . Lord, teach us to pray.*—ROMANS 8:26; LUKE 11:1

I CLOSED my sermon this morning with the announcement that the same subject would be continued tonight. In the morning sermon was discussed: (1) our Lord's prayer for the Holy Spirit to accredit him and qualify him for his work; (2) his prayer against the selfish spirit of monopoly; (3) against the spirit of carnal excitement that magnified the temporal benefits of miracles above the spiritual lessons of his kingdom; (4) his prayer before ordaining preachers; (5) that man might see the spiritual nature of his kingdom; (6) that at least his immediate disciples might have a God-revealed spiritual faith in him as the Messiah; (7) that his people might see glimpses of his glory lest they should be depressed by views of his humiliation; (8) a prayer of thanksgiving for the success of his humble ministers; and (9) that his disciples might desire to learn to pray. It is purposed tonight to continue this subject in its chronological order, being governed by the chronology observed in the *Harmony* of Dr. Broadus.

Tenth, Christ's prayer at the grave of Lazarus. We find this record in John 11:32-43:

"Then when Mary was come where Jesus was, and saw him, she fell down at his feet, saying unto him, Lord, if thou hadst been here, my brother had not died. When Jesus therefore saw her weeping and the Jews also weeping which came with her, he groaned in the spirit, and was troubled, and said, Where have ye laid him? They said unto him, Lord, come and see. Jesus wept. Then said the Jews, Behold how he loved him! And some of them said, Could not this man, which opened the eyes of the blind, have caused that even this man should not have died? Jesus therefore again groaning in himself cometh to the grave. It was a cave and a stone lay upon it. Jesus said, Take ye away the stone. Martha, the sister of him that was dead, saith unto him, Lord, by this time he stinketh, for he hath been dead four days. Jesus saith unto her, said I not unto thee that if thou wouldst believe thou shouldst see the glory of God? Then they took away the stone from the place where the dead was laid. And Jesus lifted up his eyes and said, Father, I thank thee that thou hast heard me. And I knew that thou hearest me always; but because of the people which stand by I said it, that they may believe that thou hast sent me. And when he thus had spoken he cried with a loud voice, Lazarus, come forth!"

This record evinces the extreme sensitiveness of our Lord's nature, both in sympathy with the bereaved and in indignation against unbelief. His sympathy for the bereaved is exhibited in his tender manner and words and in his tears. His indignation against unbelief is expressed twice by the words, "groaning in spirit," and "groaning in himself." The margin translates thus: "Was moved with indignation in spirit," and "being moved with indignation in himself." It is easy to see what excited his indignation. Here were Jews from Jerusalem indulging in formal mourning and condolence, and who, under this formal mourning, were cherishing bitter unbelief and hatred of him, so that he prayed in the presence of deadly hostility as well as of loving trust.

Our record tells us the object for which he prayed, that those who believed on him should see the glory of God; that they should see that glory as triumphing over death and corruption, and that this power was to be put forth that the multitude standing around might believe that he was divinely sent. Twice before we have special instances of the raising of the dead: one, a girl who had just died; another, a young man who had been dead for some time and whose body was being carried to the grave. But this remarkable instance of resurrection was after Lazarus had been dead four days, and after decay and corruption had set in.

What lesson of value, then, do we gather from the prayer that Christ offered on this occasion? Evidently this, that in the darkest sorrows of life, when those whom we love more than life are taken away from us, we may pray to see the glory of God in their protection from the victory of the grave; that we may, by faith, confidently trust their sleeping bodies to his kind and loving and ceaseless care, and that while we sorrow, we may not sorrow as those who have no hope, but may look forward to the time when our Lord himself shall return with a shout and the sound of the trumpet, bringing with him the spirits of our dead, and that at his voice our loved ones may wake up from the grave and be glorified and reunited to their spirits. We may learn from it that the same Jesus who so tenderly comforted Mary and Martha, and who wept to share their sorrow, likewise commiserates us in our days of darkness, and exercises toward us the same loving compassion that he did toward them.

Eleventh, praying for little children, Matthew 19:13-15: "Then were there brought unto him little children, that he should put his hands on them and pray: and the disciples rebuked them. But Jesus said, Suffer little children, and forbid them not, to come unto me: for of such is the kingdom of heaven. And he laid his hands on them and departed thence."

We have just seen Jesus at the grave; we now see him at the cradle. And as he could pray at the end of human existence, so now we behold him praying at its beginning. What a touching scene! See the mothers bringing their babes in their arms and asking that our Lord should put his hands on them and pray, invoking a heavenly benediction on their infant life. And mark, too, the spirit of the disciples, who would forbid such objects of prayer, and hear the rebuke of Jesus and see him as he takes the children in his arms. What

a lesson does this suggest to us! Does it not show us that
we in a measure share the spirit that animated the disciples
of Christ, and especially when we do not seem willing to pray
for any except adults, or those who have become hardened in
sin? Do we not defer our prayers too long? Why should
we not bend over the infant in the cradle before into that
young mind has ever come a knowledge of right and wrong;
before those little feet have learned to walk in the paths of
wickedness; before that chubby little hand has been clenched
to strike in malice; before those mild eyes have sparkled with
hate; before habits of evil have been formed and temptations
have been felt?

Would it not be well that we should pray that God should
guard them from the evil one and prepare them for the duties
of life and the trials of life hidden from their sight, but that
yet lie certainly before them in their path? I have myself,
not once but many times, and not in the case of my own children only, but in the case of the children of my neighbors,
knelt at the cradle and prayed that God's blessing might rest
upon the unconscious infant, and that his life and health and
spiritual prosperity might be precious in the sight of God.
Yes, brethren, pray at the cradle, pray at the grave, pray everywhere.

Twelfth, in view of the inquiry of Gentiles concerning himself, he prays that the Father may glorify his name. The record
speaks thus: (John 12:20-28) "And there were certain Greeks
among them that came up to worship at the feast. The same
came therefore to Philip, which was of Bethsaida of Galilee,
and desired him, saying, Sir, we would see Jesus. Philip cometh and telleth Andrew and again Andrew and Philip tell
Jesus. And Jesus answered them, saying, The hour is come
that the Son of man should be glorified. Verily, verily, I say
unto you, Except a corn of wheat fall into the ground and
die, it abideth alone; but if it die it bringeth forth much fruit.
He that loveth his life shall lose it; and he that hateth his
life in this world shall keep it unto life eternal. If any man

serve me, let him follow me; and where I am there shall also my servant be; if any man serve me, him will my Father honor. Now is my soul troubled; and what shall I say? Father, save me from this hour; but for this cause came I unto this hour. Father, glorify thy name. Then came there a voice from heaven saying, I have both glorified it and will glorify it again."

The Greeks are coming! "Sir, we would see Jesus." It is a presage of brighter days in the future when the wall of partition shall be broken down, when the way to heaven shall be made free to the barbarian, the Scythian, the bond, the free, yea, to every tribe and tongue; when those who had been aliens from the commonwealth of Israel, and without God, and without hope in the world, should turn toward the Lord. The Greeks are coming! "Sir, we would see Jesus." Well might he, in view of that inquiry, cry out in earnestness, "Father, glorify thy name." He glorified it when Cornelius sent for Peter. He glorified it as Paul preached at Athens and Corinth and Thessalonica and Berea and Rome and to the ends of the world. And now, when we see, wide-open, the door of access to all of the South American republics, to ancient, priest-ridden Italy and other Latin states, to Japan and China and a thousand other foreign fields, may we not say, "The Greeks are coming. Oh, Father, glorify thy name in their salvation"?

Thirteenth, he prays that Peter's faith may not fail under the sifting process of the devil. Our record says (Luke 21:31-34): "And the Lord said, Simon, Simon, behold, Satan hath desired to have you, that he may sift you as wheat: but I have prayed for thee that thy faith fail not: and when thou art converted strengthen thy brethren. And he said unto him, Lord, I am ready to go with thee, both into prison and to death. And he said, I tell thee, Peter, the cock shall not crow this day before that thou shalt thrice deny that thou knowest me."

Behold this impulsive and confident disciple, who is ready enough to admit that all other men may fall away from Christ and deny him, but he will not deny him even under the test of death. Behold the audacity of Satan and his malice and his shrewd judgment of the weakness of human nature. What audacity does he manifest in approaching the Lord Jesus Christ himself and making a special request that he might sift the followers of Christ as a man sifts wheat. See, too, that our Lord grants Satan's request. He does enable him to thoroughly test their faith by his sifting process. Judas, as chaff, is finally and forever separated from the wheat, and under his sifting, Peter, relying so confidently in his own strength, falls fearfully, falls repeatedly, falls shamefully, and yet, O matchless mercy! see the prayer of Christ intervening, lest his trust in the Lord should be utterly blotted out.

This is the only passage in the Word of God upon which the Papists rely as cited in the Vatican decrees, to prove the infallibility of the Pope. They say that Christ prayed that faith might not fail Peter; that the Pope is Peter's successor; that Peter, residing in the Pope, is still preserved from failing faith; and therefore when the Pope speaks ex-cathedra his utterances are infallible. But as was abundantly demonstrated in the famous speech of Bishop Kenrick, prepared to be delivered to the Vatican Council, the word "faith" here does not refer to the system of doctrine, nor the teaching gift, but to Peter's personal trust in our Lord. What, then, is the lesson to us? What object of prayer does it suggest? What weakness of our own does it guard us against? Certainly while it admonishes us not vainly to rely on our own powers, not to think more highly of ourselves than we ought to think, and while it exhorts that he that thinketh he standeth should take heed lest he fall, yet it abundantly shows that our salvation does not so much depend on our hold on Christ as Christ's hold on us. It shows that but for the intercession of Jesus there would not necessarily be perpetuity in our faith; that it is his love for us that prevents us from turning him loose altogether in the hour of trial.

If this be true, then certainly it is a becoming thing, an appropriate and urgent thing, that we should watch and pray against temptation, as this very Peter is exhorted to do but a short time after. It should teach us to consider how fallible and few are our human resources when pitted against principalities and powers in high places, and how little in ourselves we are able to stand when we wrestle, not against flesh and blood, but against Satan and his demons, and that if the devil had carefully studied the case of Job and formed his judgment concerning the reality of Job's religion, and believed that if the case was put into his hands, he could destroy Job's trust in God, and if he had the audacity to believe that he could shake loose from Christ the faith of his immediate disciples, what is there in us that should lead us to presume upon our powers of resistance, should the day of direful evil come upon us? How do you know, my brother, but that the fiery trials through which you are passing may have been allowed of our Lord at Satan's request? Satan, knowing your weaknesses, your susceptibilities, your vain confidence, your presumption, has asked God that he might sift you as wheat. Should not then you pray to God to be delivered from the evil one? Should it not be a matter of deep joy to you that a stronger hand than yours grasps your life? Oh, let every one of us lift up our eyes and hearts today to our great High Priest, who ever liveth to intercede for us, and put our feebleness in his hands, and say to him, "Lord, pray for me that my faith may not fail, as thou didst pray that Peter's faith might not fail."

Fourteenth, his prayer at the institution of the Supper. The record of this familiar transaction may be found in Matthew 26:27; Mark 14:22-23; Luke 22:19-20; 1 Corinthians 11:23-25. The act of devotion here is expressed by these words, "blessed," or "gave thanks," and because of his thanksgiving the Supper has been called the Eucharist, the form of the language our Lord used on private occasions as well as in this solemn hour. It applies in one sense as well to the ordinary

giving of thanks when we partake of our daily food as it does
to the institution of a solemn memorial, so that there is presented to the mind two objects of prayer: first, that we should
thank God as we partake of our daily food in our homes, in our
families, but more particularly and solemnly when we come
to that memorial ordinance established in connection with the
Passover Feast, and indeed suggested by that remarkable ancient type, that here, as a church, we should lift up our hearts
in gratitude for the atoning sacrifice of our Lord.

We see the Christ. We see his broken body. We see that
body separated from its blood. We see the double giving of
thanks for the body broken and for the blood shed, and it
should lead us in every act of our private life, but more particularly in that solemn hour when the church of God as-
sembles together to commemorate the departed Lord, our
hearts should go out in gladness and thanksgiving that the
bread of life was given to us. It may well be that we have
given to this ordinance an air of sorrow, of deep melancholy,
borrowed from the minds of the disciples, as they viewed it
as an announcement of his speedy death, but evidently he
intended it to be an occasion of joy and not of sadness. Solemn? Yes, but not such a solemnity as banishes melody from
the heart and rejoicing from the spirit. In giving thanks for
a favor, there is bound to be in the heart a feeling of joy
for that favor, else there is no gratitude in our formal word
of thanks. Our celebrations of the Lord's Supper should
therefore be occasions of great, deep, and solemn joy and not
of sadness.

Fifteenth, he prayed that another paraclete might be given to
the disciples when he departed—a Comforter. Our record says,
"I will pray the Father and he will give you another Comforter that he may be with you forever, even the Spirit of
truth whom the world cannot receive, for it beholdeth him
not, neither knoweth him; ye know him for he abideth with
you and shall be in you. I will not leave you desolate. I
come unto you" (John 14:16-18). This prayer of our Lord

was answered on the Day of Pentecost. His presence in the person of the Spirit is referred to in the commission, "Lo, I am with you alway, even to the end of the world." From the time that this prayer was answered the gospel has been preached, and wherever preached with power, has been accompanied by the Holy Ghost sent down from heaven. We need not elaborate this point, as it has been sufficiently discussed on the first prayer of Jesus for the Holy Spirit. The lesson taught here is the same. It teaches us that we cannot go out and work for God, that we cannot be happy in our work, that we cannot overcome the world, that we cannot lead men to Christ, if the Comforter be not with us. Oh, how great is our desolation, with Jesus gone, if the other Comforter be not with us!

Sixteenth, the great intercession. We now come to the Lord's prayer, not that which is usually styled "The Lord's Prayer," for that was a prayer that he intended for us to offer, but this is a prayer that our Lord himself offered. It embraces the whole of the seventeenth chapter of John, which it is not necessary for me to quote in detail. The prayers of the Bible are usually very short. This and the prayer offered by Solomon at the dedication of the Temple, are the only long prayers in the whole Book of God, and he himself specially cautioned his disciples against vain repetitions in prayer or any thought that they should be heard for their much speaking. Let us notice some of the details of this memorable prayer that our Lord offered for his disciples.

First, "Holy Father, keep in thy name what thou hast given me. While I was with them, I kept them in thy name which thou hast given me, and I guarded them, and not one of them perished. . . . I pray that thou shouldest keep them from the evil one." This first supplication of our Lord, as contained in this great intercession, evidently shows our exposedness to danger from Satan, and that if it was necessary for him to pray that Peter's faith should not fail under the sifting process of the devil, it is just as essential to our safety that the same prayer should be offered in our behalf. We need to be kept, to be kept by the power of God, to be kept through faith unto salvation. We need to be guarded. Our adversary goeth about as a roaring lion, seeking whom he may devour. His malevolence against Christians is now just as bitter and undying in its hate as it was in the days of Christ. No one of us is safe, even for one hour, if the protecting power of God should be withdrawn. It is a prayer that we should breathe out from our hearts every day of our lives, "Lord, keep me this day from the evil one." None of us, brethren, could give guarantees of the maintenance of our Christian integrity, of the preservation of our purity, of the brightness of the shining of our spiritual lamp, if the keeping power of God were withdrawn from us. When, then, you want to know for what to pray every day of your life, pray, "Father, let me not perish. Guard me. Keep me from the evil one."

What next did he pray for? Hear the words, "Sanctify them in the truth. Thy word is truth." We may well inquire just here the meaning of the term, "sanctify." As has been stated on more than one occasion, the word has several meanings. It may mean to set apart, to consecrate, or it may mean to make holy. In this connection it certainly has the former meaning, to set apart, consecrate in truth. We gather this from the following language used in the same connection: "And for their sakes I sanctify myself that they themselves also may be sanctified in truth." Whatever then was the sanctification which Christ exercised in his own case is the sanctification that he prayed for in behalf of his disciples, but as he himself was already as pure and holy as God is pure and holy, certainly he did not sanctify himself in the sense of to make holy, but to set apart himself and to consecrate himself in the truth, in doing the truth. So he prays that his people may set themselves apart and may consecrate themselves as witnesses of the truth. To set one's self apart to a particular object makes that one a devoted one. I mean by a devoted one him who has not only consecrated himself to one thing, but separated himself from all other things in order to a full consecration.

And I would here inquire, brethren, if a large part of the barrenness of our present state does not arise from the fact that in this first sense of the word "sanctify" we have not sanctified ourselves. We have not permitted God to sanctify us. We have not recognized that we are God's own people in the true sense of that word "peculiar," a peculiar people, that is, peculiar to God, belonging to God alone and to his truth alone, acknowledging no other authority, subordinating ourselves to no other government, but making him not only supreme in our life, but supreme as the object of our affections. When we remember then that Jesus prayed, "Sanctify them in the truth," let us pray that prayer. Let us endeavor by God's help to make a deliberate act of entire consecration to his service.

Did you ever do that? Did you ever go off alone and, after thoughtful consideration of the whole matter, deliberately, as if you had written the words down on a piece of paper, and signed your name to it, and placed the document upon the altar of God, in this form: "Lord Jesus Christ, I do this day (mentioning the date), here and now offer to thee myself, all of me, my entire life and being, to be thine alone, to suffer what seems good to thee, to bear what thou mayest choose to impose upon me, to do what thou wouldst have me do. Lord, take me altogether and write thy name of ownership and authority upon my head and hand and heart, all over me, as thine, forever thine." That is the sanctification that is referred to here.

Mark next that he prays in this great intercession, "that they may be one." This is certainly a prayer for the unity of his people, that as Jesus and the Father are one, so his people should be one—one Lord, one faith, one baptism, one Holy Spirit. Oh, this bond of unity! Behold how good and how pleasant it is for brethren to dwell together in unity! And whenever there is a tendency in any of us to create strife or schism, to make separations between brethren, to alienate, to divide the followers of God, let us in our shame and sorrow come back to this prayer of our Lord that they may be one. How many exhortations leap from the Word of God at a moment's thought, substantiating this prayer of Jesus, exhorting us to be of one mind, that there be no divisions, and oh, how much of shame and reproach has come upon Christ's cause by our divisions among ourselves! Why need we then say that we do not know what to pray for when there is such a glorious, broad object for prayer? "Let God grant that thy people may be one, that the world may believe that the Father did send thee." Mark again: "Father, that which thou hast given me I will that where I am, there they also may be with me, that they may behold my glory which thou hast given me."

Oh, how precious is this prayer of Jesus! We hear his words, "Let not your heart be troubled. In my Father's house are many mansions. I go to prepare a place for you, and if I go to prepare a place for you, I will come again and receive you unto myself." And how joyous the exultation of Paul in his letter to the Thessalonians: "And so we shall be ever with the Lord." How it reconciles him, not merely to the thought of dying, but makes departure a thing to be desired, so as actually to place him in the attitude of wishing to depart, knowing that death is gain, because when absent from the body he is present with the Lord. While we hold the cold hands of the dying saint and mark the death struggle as the spirit is separating from the body, and shudder at the physical contortions that mark the dissolution of the bond that held the dual nature of man together, ought not our souls to rejoice at the thought that in a moment's time this fleeting spirit shall be with God? "Lord Jesus, receive my spirit." Well might the apostle say, "For we know that when the earthly house of this tabernacle is dissolved, we have a building of God, a house not made with hands, eternal in the heavens." Yes, we may always pray for that, Lord, to be with thee. Whom have I in heaven but thee, and who is there on earth that I desire beside thee? And to behold that glory and to share that glory, who can estimate it? Eye hath not seen, ear hath not heard, nor the heart of man conceived of the things which God has in reservation for those that love him. True, he makes a revelation concerning them by the Holy Spirit to his people, but it is a revelation that the mind can but faintly grasp. It is far different from the actual fruition itself.

Notice finally under this great intercession this prayer: "That the love wherewith thou lovedst me may be in them and I in them." What a love is this! The love of the Father for the Son. "Oh, love divine, all love excelling!" And yet Jesus prayed that this love might be in us—the love that the Father had for him, the love of God, shed abroad in our hearts by the Holy Ghost, given unto us. If after cold, dark winter has bound the earth in its rigorous chains, the sunshine of spring shall come, and the falling rains, melting the snow, warming the heart of the earth and causing it to bud and blossom and bear fruit, clothing its prairies with carpets of grass and its forests with foliage, and filling the boughs of the trees with the singing of birds, oh, what must be the effect in us of the love that God had for our Lord Jesus Christ! And yet he prays that that love may be in us.

But mark you the connection: "That the love wherewith thou lovedst me may be in them and I in them." "I in them," which shows that if Christ is not formed in our hearts the hope of glory, if on our souls is not impressed the image of Christ, then the Father cannot love us as he loved the Son. But if in each of us is the reproduction of the image of the Son, then the same love that was extended to the Son will be extended to us. How hard to realize that thought, that even in me, so prone to sin, so fallible in judgment, so erring— even in me, shall be the image of Christ, and because of that image there shall be in me the same love of the Father that was extended to our Lord.

Seventeenth, his prayer in Gethsemane: "Father, if it be possible, let this cup pass from me." As it is my purpose to use the import of this prayer in connection with another to be considered later, I will pass it for the moment and consider next:

Eighteenth, his prayer for sinners. The record says (Luke 23:33-34), "And there they crucified him and the malefactors, one on the right hand and the other on the left. And Jesus said, Father, forgive them, they know not what they do." This voice of Christ from the cross possesses for me a very deep significance. This is not our Lord praying for those who are Christians. Unquestionably, it is our Lord praying for sinners, and he is praying that their sins may be forgiven them, and we have abundant evidence that many of them were forgiven, from the subsequent testimony of the Acts of the Apostles. Even those that crucified the Lord of Glory, in the day of the Spirit's power, were pricked to the heart, and cried out, "Men and brethren, what shall we do?" and by the grace of God were saved by that very blood which with wicked hands they had shed. This prayer of Jesus is an everlasting warrant to his church and people to pray for sinners. When I look at it, when I reflect on it, I cannot help but recall the words of good old Samuel, when the sinners of Israel asked him not to cease praying for them. He replied, "God forbid that I should so sin as to cease to pray for you." While the world stands, and the memory of the cross abides, it must ever be a lesson that cannot be blotted out, that Christian people who love to walk in the tracks of our Lord Jesus Christ and observe his example, may pray for forgiveness of sinners.

Nineteenth, "My God, my God, why hast thou forsaken me?" (Matthew 27:46). As was stated just now, this dying exclamation of our Lord must be considered in connection with the prayer offered in Gethsemane. In the one case the shadow of the approaching death, the anticipation of the ignominy of dying a felon's death, not as a martyr, but dying as a sinner, because in the place of sinners—I say that the apprehension of this despising shame, of this darkness, was so great that he cried out, "My Father, if it be possible, let this cup pass from me." And here he offers the prayer of one who is lost: "Why hast thou forsaken me?" It is the wail of a lost soul, because he was standing in the place of a lost soul. He was undergoing the execution of a culprit. The sword had been *awaked* against the shepherd and he was smitten. On him were falling the thunderbolts of the divine wrath. He was made to be sin, though he knew no sin, and it is maintained that in this moment, in this hour of supernatural darkness, which lasted three hours, when all earthly and heavenly light was shut out from him, that at this moment he died the spiritual death. To die spiritually is to be separated from God, and so unspeakably awful was the horror of that separation, when he thus tasted spiritual death, there was extorted from his anguished lips the cry, "My God, my God, why hast thou forsaken me?"

These are not prayers, I trust, that we are to offer. We do not have to drink that cup. But they do have a very solemn lesson for the unconverted. As Jesus felt in Gethsemane, and as he felt when the Father forsook him, so must feel every impenitent man when he dies. Then he tastes spiritual death. Then he enters that outer darkness. Then he shrinks with unspeakable horror from the cup that is filled with the wrath of God. But it is pressed to his lips, and if he be out of Christ, he must drink it. And if it was not possible for God's omniscience to discover any other way to save a sinner, nor for his omnipotence to provide any other way except through the vicarious death of Jesus Christ; if to save any sinner Jesus had to drink that cup, had to be separated from the Father, whoever does not accept the atonement of Jesus Christ must drink that cup for himself and bear that separation for himself; must hear the word, "Depart, ye accursed, into everlasting fire prepared for the devil and his angels." The Scripture says that he tasted death for every man. It does not refer to the mere dissolution of soul and body. It means that he tasted spiritual death, and thus was his body offered on the altar of his divinity, and when he died that spiritual death and said, "It is finished," that was the end of the expiation. All else that followed was but the carrying out and completing of the work which had been done. His resurrection, his ascension into heaven, his enthronement there, his ever living to make intercession for us—all of it is based upon the expiation that he made on Calvary.

Twentieth, we come now to the last prayer of Jesus. "Father, into thy hands I commend my spirit" (Luke 24:44). That this has a suggestive lesson is evident from the fact that the disciples after this time adopted it as a form of prayer for themselves when in the act of dying. We see it illustrated in the case of Stephen, who, looking steadfastly up into heaven, saw the heavens open, saw Jesus standing at the right hand of the Majesty on high, and kneeling down and speaking to his blessed Lord in full view, and imitating his Lord's last prayer, he said, "Lord Jesus, receive my spirit." I have read of a mother who was bending over her dying child. He had been sinful. He was suffering terribly. Every breath was anguish. Spasms shook his frame and he kept appealing to his mother: "Oh, Mother, where am I going? Mother, who will meet me on the other side of death?" And his mother kept saying, "Son, oh, my dying boy, say this: 'Lord Jesus, receive my spirit!' "

IV

CHRIST'S DYING PRAYER

Text: *Then Jesus said, Father, forgive them for they know not what they do.*—Luke 23:34.

THERE are three thoughts in the text: When he offered this prayer, or the circumstances under which the petition fell from his lips; next, the petition itself; and third, the reason assigned for it in the text with an application of the principles involved in the several thoughts in tracing out that prayer to see what became of it.

I have been enabled a number of times in my life to genuinely pray for my enemies. I do not think there was ever a case where I did not sooner or later bring myself to the point that I could really and sincerely and earnestly pray to God to forgive them. But I confess here and now that I have never been able so to pray at such a time as marked this prayer, "Father, forgive them!"

When does he say it? Right in the commission of the injury. Right at the time the indignity was the freshest and hottest; when they had placed him between two thieves; these are the associations; when they crucified him; when they had written an accusation over his head; when they were pointing their fingers at him; when there had not yet been wiped from his face the saliva they so shamelessly spat upon his cheek; when the pain was yet in his head where the hair had been rudely jerked out; when the thorns were yet on his brow, and when the scorn and gibing and jeering and slander and slime were poured out on him; then, he said, "Father, forgive them." I confess I could not have done it. It is a sublime exhibition of the divinity of Jesus Christ. When the martyrs, like Stephen, offered such prayers, they were sustained by him. They saw him standing to approve and encourage.

Now, the second point: What was it he asked? He asked
that God would forgive that offense against him; that he
would not lay it to their charge; that he would provide for a
pardon; that he would stay the sword of divine justice; that
he would lay the hand of restraint upon the quivering thunder-
bolt of his wrath, ready to smite such an offender. Forgive
them! Blot this out! Hold it not against them!

I ask you to look at that and I ask you if the earth could
have furnished any such demonstration of divinity as that. I
have often considered the prayer that he taught us to pray,
in which he says: "After this manner pray ye: Forgive us
our sins, or debts, or trespasses, as we forgive them that sin
against us."

It is the most searching lesson to which the human mind
could be directed. Can you offer that prayer? Are you willing to place your own case in as much jeopardy as your heart
prompts you to put the case of an offender against yourself?
Are you willing to say deliberately, "Lord, God, be merciful to
me as I have been merciful. If I have taken my enemy by
the throat in my mind and said, 'Pay me what thou owest';
if I have in my imagination delighted in the thought of his
downfall; if his misery and anguish have seemed to me as a
pleasing thing to think about as it lies out in the future before
me, can I say, 'Lord, God, do me that way'?"

The forgiveness of sins! It is the essence and basis of salvation. It is that which makes the name of Jesus the sweetest
name on the earth, because it is only through him, by him and
on account of what he has done, that any of us can ever be
forgiven. Sometimes—not often, but sometimes—we do get
into a state of mind that strips us of our self-importance, that
divests us of our conceit, that is stern and just enough in self-
examination and self-judgment to strip us of self-pity, and
when we get in that condition (and we never get there unless
led by the Spirit of God), there never has been a man of us,
or a woman of us, or a child of us, when there, but will say,

"The thing that I need more than everything else in this world is forgiveness. I am a sinner! I am a sinner!"

There is something about sin that is very defiling. It is a slimy thing, and contact with it, and especially when it lingers and we cannot divest ourselves of it, or of its loathsomeness, eats into our hearts, corrupts the fountains of purity and takes away from us the dignity of manhood and gives us the image, not only of beasts, but of devils.

There is also in it, when we look at it as to its consequences to ourselves, a persuasion that deepens as time lengthens, that we must meet the judgment—a thought of it, not only with reference to the penalty to be imposed upon ourselves, but in its far-reaching consequences to others, and to those entirely innocent of the offense.

Let a man sin and he cannot terminate it in himself. To save his life he cannot keep the weight and burden and consequences of it from resting on his wife, on his child, on the unconscious babe sleeping in its mother's arms. He cannot throw the shadow of that sin off the cradle of his infant. He cannot dispel the shadow of that sin from his own grave, nor can he drive it from the future of those that are nearest and dearest to him.

Sin is the abominable thing that God hates, and the only thing that he does hate in the world. And hear, "Father, forgive them, forgive them!" Would you exchange it for this, "Father, give them long life! Father, make them rich! Father, put their hands on the neck of their enemies"? O what possession conceivable to the human mind, what conception that the heart of man can entertain, is comparable to the richness of the forgiveness of God! Forgiveness!

That does not mean that you have deserved it. That does not mean that you have bought it. That does not mean that there is a measure of good in you on account of other things, that by an equalization, striking a balance, will entitle you to it. But mercy, grace, forgiveness! And forgiveness how long and how far? Forgiveness forever! And how many times? Seventy times seven! There is something in the subject of the forgiveness of sins as represented in this prayer of Jesus Christ, that to me holds up the excellency of his divine character, the necessity and the richness of his sacrifice more than everything else in the Bible.

Now, the last point of the text before we come to the application: "Father, forgive them, for they know not what they do." Let us consider that somewhat. Does that mean that by ignorance we are justified? Does that mean that ignorance is a sufficient extenuation or palliation of an offense? It means this, so much and no more, that to the extent that it has blinded the offender it is a pardonable case under the conditions provided in the gospel. That is all that it means.

Did you ever read in the Bible where Jesus Christ prayed for the devils? Is there one hint that these intelligences, who once peopled heaven and sinned knowingly and wilfully and maliciously—that any provision was made for their pardon?

Can you show me anywhere in the Bible where a man by processes of self-degradation, by constant hardening of heart, by continual departure from God, goes on until at last he sins against the Holy Ghost, against spiritual light and knowledge, may yet claim the benefit of this prayer, "Father, forgive them, for they know not what they do"?

Unquestionably the apostle put this identical interpretation on it when he carried the message of life and salvation to those very men who had heaped these indignities so undeservedly upon the Son of God. He says, "I wot, brethren, that through ignorance ye did it, as did also your rulers."

This leads us into a line of thought that, it seems to me, deserves more than usual care and attention. How much of what is done here on this earth, by men, is covered by their ignorance? To what extent has the lack of spiritual knowledge placed them inside of the possibilities, inside of the orbit of the influence of this prayer for forgiveness? I am sure there must be some way to understand it.

Let us not, however, try to measure this ignorance as palliating offenses against ourselves. The trouble about that case is our selfishness; and our desire to see vengeance meted out against the offender will not permit us to admit enough of ignorance in the case. But let us take a case wherein we have been the offenders, wherein we have done things that are obnoxious to the divine law, wherein we have trampled upon the rights of our fellow men, wherein we have rudely and cruelly wounded the feelings of the innocent.

Now when it comes to such a case, I am sure each of us will say, "I did not thoroughly understand it. It was not altogether intentionally done. I did not have full light on the subject. Doubtless I saw some of it, but I did not get all its bearings. Indeed, do not make me out that kind of a criminal; surely I am not that bad. Is thy servant a dog to do such things? If I had known even as much as I know now, if I had occupied a higher standpoint of observation, if I had had a broader sweep of vision, so that I could have made due allowance for the influences which had been at work upon this enemy of mine, which led him to do the thing that provoked this wrong upon my part, why, I am sure that I would not have hit quite so hard. O just think of the things I did not see! Just think of how short is my view of the past or future! I am sure I had no realization that consequences would keep on and on and on until they struck the shores of eternity. If I knew it theoretically, I did not realize it. Ignorance, Lord, ignorance! Let me be in that orbit of possibility! It was not all malice, it was not all intent upon my part to do such a thing."

Ah, we do make fine pleaders, when it comes to our own cases, and we stand with our self-pity, described in one of the matchless poems of old, where a man walking down the aisles at night over the cold marble floor of a silent church, was so touched by compassion on himself that he fell to weeping and wondering that God and angels and men had not seen how much he deserved pity.

On one occasion God said to David: "You have done a great wrong. Now which will you take—that I shall judge you or that I shall turn you over to your enemies?" "Lord God, you judge me! You judge me! Never turn me over to a man to judge me. Never turn me over to an enemy, and let him tell what I owe. Never let him be the one that is to trace the secret workings of my mind, and to paint just exactly the object that I had in view in everything that I did and said. Not mine enemy! Let me fall into thy hands, O God!"

And I do not hesitate to say that if I stand before the judgment bar of God, knowing omnipotence, knowing omniscience, knowing omnipresence, knowing the eternity of hell, knowing that from that fiat when once spoken there would be no recovery, I would say, "Lord, God, you speak my sentence."

Now I will make the application. Studying such a prayer as that, the prayer itself, the tremendous thing asked for, studying the time and circumstances under which that prayer was offered, studying the vast charity of the mind that supposed, that took for granted, that there were some unforeseen, mitigating circumstances to be reckoned to the offender; that he did not have full and complete light; that there were some influences operating upon him, perhaps, that he inherited, some coming from the side pressure of others, something that came under the general name of ignorance, and that stripped the deed of entire devilishness and malice—I say, looking at that prayer under those three conditions of it, I have an intense longing to see what became of it.

Once I was reading a history, you have read the history doubtless, a very famous one, an ancient history in which the historian with a graphic power that I have never known to be surpassed, describes a struggle made by a free people for the maintenance of their liberties—describes the young hero that led them in conflict against the terrible odds of the conquerors of the world; describes them as they brought their bare breasts, exposed to dart and arrow, and placed

them against the iron-sheathed bodies of their enemies, and at
last the interest is keyed up higher and higher until you see
that glorious young hero take his position on a bridge in a
river, until it seems that every eye, above and below, is fixed,
and right there, without another scratch of the pen, the historian stopped, and there is not a man living that knows the
sequel of it; it stops right there on that bridge.

Well, I cannot describe to you how that thing used to af-
fect me. I wanted to read the rest of it. I wanted to see
what became of that hero. I wanted to know the end of that
story. But there the historian's volume ended and no successor from either side completed the story. But the interest
that I felt in watching the conclusion of that patriotism, of
that unflinching heroism, of bringing that undisciplined and
unpanoplied valor to fight bravely, triumphantly, against the
ironclad and invincible phalanx whose eagles had soared and
screamed over the capitals of the world, that is an infinitesimal
thought beside the interest that was in my heart to see what
became of this prayer, such a prayer as this, a prayer offered
under such circumstances. What did become of it?

There is a story of a little child in a boat with its father
and mother, gliding down a gentle stream, until suddenly
it brought them to a lake covered with lilies, and from the
lilies of the lake, and from its strange loneliness, suddenly a
huge, beautiful, strangely beautiful white bird rose up and
gradually floated out of sight in the blue sky, and the child
stared at the vacancy in space and said, "Mother, where did
the bird go?"

So would I inquire of this white-winged bird, this purest
utterance that in time of awful trial ever fell from lips that
were called human, what did become of this prayer? It rises
amid the groans of the one who offered it. It rises in the
thick pall of darkness that surrounded him. It rises from
the midst of the anguish of his physical, mental, and spiritual
suffering. It rises above the head of the mob that had sought
and had obtained his death warrant. It rises above the clouds

that floated serenely and unthinkingly by, and above the cold, pitiless stars that have looked tranquilly down on human suffering since human eyes caught their sparkle until now, and it went out of human sight, lost —lost in the dim distance of the skies above. What became of that prayer? It has gone out of sight like the bird.

But I turn over here to another book. Men have lost sight of the prayer. When they quit thinking about the prayer, a very faulty man got up to preach a sermon, and under the influence of that sermon three thousand men and women of the murderers are forgiven. There comes from the throne of mercy, from the home of the divine beneficence—there comes a swift-winged messenger, not where a lonely and solitary criminal is awaiting the execution of the death penalty, but where a multitude of men and women are under sentence of death, and there are three thousand pardoned in one day— three thousand souls forgiven in one day.

And shall the preacher say, "What a work I have done today, what a work!" Was it the preacher? I tell you it was the prayer that had been forgotten. It was the petition that the sufferer himself offered in his dying agony: "Father, forgive them, for they know not what they do." It was that petition that pierced the skies and moved the heart of God and interposed the arm of Omnipotence and brought down peace and salvation to the murderers of the Lord Jesus Christ.

It will be, it seems to me—I do not know, but it seems to me—that when we get to heaven, one of the most curious and at the same time one of the most entertaining and one of the most profitable employments of that blessed estate will be to take up the books and from each event read back and trace its cause.

How many a one will find that he has crowned himself for what he is entitled to no credit at all! There will be seen what became of the white birds of prayer. There will be seen, mapped out plainly in God's unerring book, that humble piety, unrecorded piety, so far as earthly records are concerned, has said in the solitude of some night, "Lord, God, forgive that sinner!"

I stand absolutely overwhelmed in the presence of the sweetness and of the power of genuine prayer. Prayer! I can understand when I turn over and read the apostle's extreme solicitude when he writes to this man and that man, and this church and that church, asking favors. What does he ask for? Every time one thing seems to him to be more important than everything else. It is this, "Brethren, pray for me. Pray for me! Brethren, when you meet at the church, when at night you kneel down by your bedside, when God's eye is upon you, pray for me. Pray for me that I may be kept from evil. Pray for me that I may have strength in preaching the truth of God. Pray for me!"

O thou greatest of all the gifts of a loving heart to a friend, prayer, thou art the sweetest and best! I do not want to say it so much that it will become commonplace, but I know I do feel it. I will never be able to make you know what effect has been produced upon my mind sometimes when I have been lying sick and somebody comes home and stands by the bed and says, "O you ought to have heard them pray for you tonight!"

Are you a sinner, a lost sinner? Then you ask men to do this. Go up to them and say, "Brethren, pray for me. O send up a petition to the throne of God's mercy, that my sins may be blotted out." Just that.

Now I have just this to add. I do not know how to bring it about. I am sure you do not. But whenever you can get a congregation of Christians fully to realize what tremendous power there is in prayer, whenever you can get that congregation united in mind and all bowed down together and saying, "Lord God, send a revival; send convicting and converting grace among the people," then when you get through, and you are a member of that congregation, and you catch that spirit, and you feel it on you, there begin to run through you thrills just like the sensations under a galvanic battery.

You do not know what is the matter with you. You begin to feel an uplifting of the mind, an exaltation of the spirit, a glorification. You begin to see all the worldly things that had charmed you fade into nothingness, and heaven comes down and gets nearer and closer until you can catch the luster upon its golden spires, and until you can inhale the fragrance of its atmosphere, and until your own soul is illumined by its splendor, and until you say, "I am in direct touch with God." It is the grandest experience in the world. That is the conquering church. Go trace the prayer of Jesus.

I talked with an old man once and asked him if certain Scriptures were at all times equally profitable to him, and he said not; that sometimes certain passages were very precious, but at other times he could not get hold of them. But he said, "Here is one that I can always put my finger on. It is where Jesus is offering his intercessory prayer for his disciples, and when he says, 'I pray not for these alone, but for all who shall believe on me through their words.' Now, I have believed on him. He is praying for me, the High Priest that liveth forever, the High Priest that does not die, the High Priest on whose garments the bells never cease to tinkle, the High Priest whose lips never become husky with pleading, the High Priest in heaven, pleading his own blood and the fulness of his own sacrifice before his own Father and in behalf of those who have been washed in his blood." That is one of the grandest thoughts and one of the most comforting in all the scheme of redemption. He prayed, and is now praying for us. He ever liveth to make intercession for us.

I want to ask you today when you go home to read the three Scriptures I have read to you this morning, and then, as each precept is called over by your lips, ask yourself this: "Can I do it? Can I do that? Isn't it better for me to do that?" If ever you should take vengeance in your hands and strike an enemy down to death, there will come a time when you will look at him smitten, and his wife smitten, and his children smitten, and his friends smitten, and when you see how powerless he lies, no longer able to lift his hand or to open his lips and speak a word, the dawnlessness and the helplessness of death, and you will look up and say, "Lord God, I would give a world if I had not struck that blow." Give place to wrath—let God do the judging.

V

SOME LIMITATIONS OF PRAYER

TEXT: *If ye shall ask anything in my name, I will do it.*
—JOHN 14:14.

I RECEIVED a letter yesterday from a pastor in the far West, stating how much his mind was troubled by this passage of Scripture. He did not know what to do with it. The promise looked to him to be too broad. He did not know to what extent he could check on it as a deposit placed in the bank of God's grace to his credit.

In replying to his letter the thought came to me that a great many other people might be similarly troubled, and as the promise follows and connects with the institution of the Lord's Supper, which we are to observe today in commemoration of his death, I thought it proper to select this passage of Scripture as a lesson and to expound it for the benefit of three classes.

The first class are pious people, who, when they look at a promise as broad as this, "If ye shall ask anything in my name, I will do it," fear that there are more limitations in it than there are, and hence the promise is to them of little practical utility.

The second class are foolish and fanatical people, who take this promise in an absolute and limitless sense, and offer prayers under it that are vain and presumptuous, tempting God.

The third class are the skeptical people, who take a broad promise like this and, first denying any limitation to it in the world, deny that there is any fulfilment of it, and hence any power in prayer based on it.

The first step toward exposition is to clear the text, that is, to ascertain just what our Lord said. When we know what he said we may proceed to inquire into its meaning. According to the Vatican and Sinaitic manuscripts, the oldest two, and many others, the true text is this: "If ye shall ask me anything in my name, I will do it," inserting the word "me" and thus making our Lord himself the person petitioned. It is probable that the transcribers of later manuscripts left out this word in copying, because of difficulties in their own minds based on internal grounds. At least, it is quite easy to see how they may have been much more influenced to omit it than to retain it.

These difficulties based on internal grounds are fourfold. 1. To insert "me" appears to make our text contradict a subsequent saying of our Lord in this same discourse, namely, "In that day ye shall ask me nothing" (John 16:23). 2. To make it further contradict that subsequent saying which specifies the "Father" as the one to whom petitions should be offered (John 16:23). 3. An impropriety is alleged against asking anything of Jesus "in his own name." 4. Prayer should not be addressed to Jesus in heaven, but always to "our Father which art in heaven" and "in the name" of Jesus. These internal grounds of objection are formidable in appearance only, and disappear when carefully examined.

Let us consider them *seriatim*. First, there is no contradiction in the Greek, between our amended text: "If ye shall ask me anything," and the first clause of John 16:23, "In that day ye shall ask me nothing." Our translation makes the contradiction by making "ask" the rendering of two different words of distinct meanings. In the first is *aitesete*, meaning to pray to, in the second *erotesete*, meaning to ask a question. The context of the second (John 16:18-19) explains its limited sense. The disciples were very desirous to ask a question of Jesus, but were afraid. They wanted an explanation of his saying, "A little while, and ye shall not see me"; and again, "and a little while, and ye shall see me." He answers their masked question, but reminds them of a time near at hand when they could ask him no questions, for he would be away

in heaven, and hence they must carry such questions to the
"other Paraclete," the Holy Spirit, who would be present.
When, therefore, he says, "In that day ye shall ask *(erotesete)*
me nothing" (that is, no questions), there is no contradiction
of "if ye shall ask *(aitesete)* me anything," (that is, offer any
petition to me in heaven).

Second, it is true that John 16:23 specifies the Father as
the one to be addressed in prayer, in Christ's name, and the
Greek verb and pronoun implied correspond, to-wit, "He will
give it you" *(dosei)*. But just in the same way, in John 14:13,
the Greek verb, agreeing with an implied pronoun of the
first person, demands the insertion of the "me," to-wit, "If ye
ask me anything this will I do" *(touto poieso)*. The verb,
in each case, clearly shows the person addressed in prayer.
If you ask the Father he will give it—if ye ask me, I will
do it.

Third, there is no impropriety in praying to Jesus in his
own name, when we consider the meaning of "in my name."
In this connection it invokes the virtue and merit of what he
had done as the basis of prayer. That is, if ye ask me anything, basing your request upon my atoning, substitutionary
sacrifice, I will do it. But if you ask me anything disregarding
my vicarious suffering as the ground of petition, I will not do
it. That would be to stultify myself. "In his name" is equivalent to "for Christ's sake" when connected with prayer; and
"for Christ's sake" means "for what Christ has done"; for
example, "God for Christ's sake has forgiven you" (Ephesians
4:32).

Fourth, to deny that prayers should be offered to Christ in
heaven, is to deny that he is God and contradicts both Scripture and history. Dying Stephen offers two prayers directly to
Jesus in heaven: "Lord Jesus, receive my spirit—Lord, lay
not this sin to their charge" (Acts 7:59-60). Twice in the
ninth chapter of Acts is stated the custom of the disciples to
"call on the name of Jesus" (verses 14 and 21). Indeed, their
praying to Jesus was the distinguishing mark of a disciple

enabling their persecutors to identify them. With this established custom agree the following Scriptures: "Arise and be baptized calling on the name of the Lord" (Acts 22:16) ; "For whosoever shall call upon the name of the Lord shall be saved" (Romans 10:13).

Nor will it do to limit these to initial invocations connected with baptism or the first confession. These prayers to Jesus distinguished the early Christians throughout their lives, as appears from Paul's address: "Unto the church of God which is at Corinth, to them that are sanctified in Christ Jesus, called to be saints, with all that in every place call upon the name of Jesus Christ our Lord, both theirs and ours."

The history of the followers of Christ, from the close of the canon of Scripture down to the present, shows that they offered both prayer and praise to Christ. As I recall it from memory, there is some reference to this custom in the famous letter of Pliny, the Younger, to the Emperor Trajan.

Having thus settled the text, "If ye shall ask me anything in my name, I will do it," let us expound it. You will observe that "anything" is very broad. But it is not limitless. The context limits it. These limitations now demand attention. The first limitation is suggested by the connection with the twelfth verse, indicated by the conjunction "and." Let us see what that conjunction is. "He that believeth on me, the works that I do he shall do also, and greater works than these shall he do," and "If ye shall ask me anything in my name, I will do it."

Evidently the petitions here have a connection with the works that the believer is commanded and expected to do. It does not mean, if I shall ask the Lord anything about building a house, that he will make an answer to it. But here is a commission given me as a Christian and to Christ's people as a church, to go out and do work, great work, greater works than he himself did, and in the performance of these works, if there rise up from their low standpoint of observation what seem to be insuperable difficulties, at such a juncture,

what are they to do? He says, "Ask me. Any petition that
you present to me, fairly relating to the performance of the
work I have commanded you to do, I will answer it; I will
do it."

Let us illustrate this. We are commanded to carry the gospel to the whole world, and we find a certain section of the
world in a certain period of the world barred against the reception of the gospel. A missionary tries to go to Japan, and
when he gets to the shore of that country he is turned away.
Here is a difficulty in doing the works that God commanded
him to do. And Jesus says, "If you will ask me anything in
my name about this work that I have commanded you to do,
I will do it for you." "Then, Lord, let this barrier be removed, and let the light of the gospel shine into Japan." And
it was removed. And so it has been in hundreds of other
instances.

The gospel is given to us to be delivered to the people for
their salvation. I see a man toward whom my heart feels
strangely drawn, and I want him to be converted. I want to
talk to him about Jesus, but I have no opportunity to talk to
him. If I call at his house, there the requirements that govern hospitality are such that I cannot readily get at the subject. If I go to his office, he is absorbed in his business and
I cannot get to talk to him on the subject. But I want to present the subject to him, the gospel of Jesus Christ, and I am
commanded to present the gospel to him. In doing the work that
the Master has commanded me to do, I find a difficulty, and
this promise says to me: "If you will ask anything in my
name, to enable you to do anything touching the duty that I
have laid upon you, I will do it." Then I say, "Lord, open
the way for me to get to that man." Well, he will do it. The
promise will be fulfilled. It is that limitation to which I wished
to call your attention first.

I ask you to notice in the second place, that the help of
Christ, the "I will do it," is based upon his going to the
Father. He says so. "Because I go to my Father." He is

discussing a state of affairs when he is no longer in the world. He is showing how, after he leaves the world, he may be continually approached in prayer by people on the very ground that he is not in the world, but has gone to the Father.

What is the force of that ground? In going to the Father there is necessary a resurrection from the dead on his part. The resurrection demonstrates him to be the Son of God with power. There is necessary an ascension of his risen body into heaven, and when that risen body reaches heaven, it is taught directly and implied inferentially that there in the holy of holies he goes and sprinkles his own blood, presents his own obedience unto death as a substitute, as a vicarious offering, and that obedience is the ground, the merit, upon which petitions are presented. Not only so, but he is up there as King of kings and Lord of lords, and as an ever living High Priest he may be approached for his people.

"Now because I go to my Father through the glorious portals of the resurrection, through the glorification of my body, through my ascent into the highest heavens, through my enthronement there as King of kings and Lord of lords, through the atonement which I there make by offering the blood shed upon the altar of earth, and through my ever living as High Priest, I will do what you ask me."

Don't you see at once that this suggests another limitation? The help that is sought in prayer, the difficulty which we propose to have removed by petition, as the removal of it is accomplished by the power that arises from the resurrection, ascension of Jesus Christ and atonement which he makes in heaven, and his enthronement as King of kings and Lord of lords, and his intercession as High Priest at the very right hand of the Majesty on high, the very thing that our petition asks for must relate to those very things. It must not be anything incongruous with that. I have no right to call upon Jesus Christ to do a thing because he has gone to the Father; that is totally out of harmony with the merit upon which that petition is to be granted.

Notice in the next place, the prayer must be in the name of Jesus. If you want to have your mind confused very much as to the import of "in my name" in this connection, read what the commentators say, most of them. Evidently there can be but one ruling signification of that phrase in any given connection. "In the name of Jesus" here must mean by virtue of the merit accruing from what Jesus did.

To illustrate: I want to check upon a bank and I have no money myself in the bank, but I want to check in view of a deposit made by somebody else. You will see at once that if the check is drawn in the name of the other man, it must not go beyond what the other man has deposited, and it must be governed by the reasons which prompted that deposit.

If I deny that the Lord Jesus Christ made a sacrifice for men, if I deny his divinity, if I deny that he was my substitute, if I deny that on Calvary he was accursed for me, how then can I go to him and ask anything in his name? "In his name" refers back to the transactions performed here upon the earth, and the phrase covers the whole ground of the merit upon which the petition is based. Of course, that suggests a limitation: That if I am to avail myself of a promise, which promise cannot be more extensive than the predicate upon which the promise itself rests, therefore I must not ask for things out of harmony with what was done by the Lord Jesus Christ, certainly not in his name.

Notice another limitation: The text says, "That will I do, that the Father may be glorified in the Son." The end to which everything points, the object had in view by the thing, measures the scope of it, and if I am to present a petition to the Lord Jesus Christ based upon that promise, there must be a connection between my petition and the end to be accomplished by the granting of the petition. Well, what is that end? That end is to glorify the Father in the Son. So when I come to offer a prayer under this promise, let me ask the question: If this prayer were granted, would it further that end? Would it bear in that direction?

Suppose I ask the Lord Jesus Christ to let me find money enough to build a marble front house, what relation is there between that marble front house and the glory of the Father in Jesus Christ? And if there be no relation between the thing asked and the end to be accomplished by the performance of the thing, the incongruity of it evidently suggests a limitation of the promise. As James puts it, "Ye ask, and receive not, because ye ask amiss, that ye may consume it on your lusts" (James 4:3). Hence I say that foolish persons, fanatical persons, will take a promise such as this, "If ye ask anything in my name, I will grant it," and assume that it means that if I ask the Lord Jesus Christ to convert this wooden chair into an iron bedstead, under this promise he is bound to do it. Not at all. It is in no sense implied by the context, nor by the things which govern the intent of the Lord Jesus Christ when he makes the promise.

I go to him with the petition. I must ask my heart, "Will the granting of that petition glorify God in Jesus Christ? Suppose it be denied me, will it interfere in the least with the glory of the Father in Jesus Christ?" Suppose I ask him, "Open a door by which the church may preach the gospel in Thibet, a country hitherto closed in by impassable barriers." I plead, "Lord, you have said, 'If you will ask anything in my name, I will do it.' I understand that this applies to anything that will help to carry out the work that you have commanded us to do, and you have commanded us to carry this gospel into Thibet, and I find here a barrier in the way of carrying the gospel there."

If that barrier is removed and the gospel is carried there and those people are saved, that will glorify the Father in the Son, the end had in view by the petition, by the promise, by the Word. Without any hestitation you may kneel down before those barriers, and with boldness lay the confident hand of faith upon the promise of God, and plead it, and claim it, and check on it, without the slightest doubt as to whether the draft will be honored.

Notice again the verse right after the text, the 15th: "If ye love me keep my commandments, and I will pray the Father and he shall give you another Comforter." Now here are two limitations suggested. Go back for a moment: "If ye shall ask anything—" "ye." Who? Does that mean anybody? Go back a little further: "He that believeth on me, the works that I do he shall do also and greater works than these shall he do." "If ye," (ye believers), "if ye believers, having in you the spirit of obedience to my commandments, shall ask me anything." "If ye love me, keep my commandments."

Now let us apply that. I say to the Lord Jesus Christ, "I offer this distinct prayer, that you will remove the barriers to the reception of the gospel in Thibet"; but suppose that while praying I am not showing my faith by my works; I am not showing that I love the Lord Jesus Christ by attempting to do what he commands me to do; but lying inert, without a motion upon my part to do the things which he has commanded me to do, and offering a prayer not for divine help to do impossible things, but to cover my own idleness. Jesus Christ despises my petition.

But a prayer in the way of duty, a prayer when you are trying to do the thing that you are commanded to do, a prayer when the spirit of obedience is on you, and you have done all you can according to the best light before you, and you are baffled by more than mortal obstacles, why, that prayer is always answered.

But suppose I say, "I will make no sort of effort to carry the gospel to Thibet, none at all; I will just fold my arms and say that when the good time comes the Lord will open the door and the Lord will carry it there and the Lord's people then can pray to him and he will open the door." The Lord will not answer such a prayer, nor does this promise cover any such a petition. "If ye love me, keep my commandments; and I will send you another Paraclete, the Holy Spirit."

What a strange thing, the conception some people have of prayer! It is just about the same as some people have about the church, that it is an ingenious contrivance prepared by the Lord Jesus Christ to prevent the accomplishment of his ends, and so they think that prayer is another device which God gives to encourage human idleness and to bring about a state of deadly moral inertia and that will be a premium upon sleep, and that will say to the man that shuns to do what God tells him to do, "Why, all you have to do is just to pray." So the miser shuts his eyes when the box for mission contributions approaches him, but sings the louder, "Fly abroad, thou mighty gospel!"

Now let us look at the other limitation suggested here: "And I will pray the Father and he will send you another Comforter." "When you wanted to know what to do while I was with you, you asked me. After I go away, when you want to know what to do, you ask him." You come to a difficulty, and hard by the difficulty is a promise, and if the Lord Jesus Christ were present, you would say to Jesus, "Here is a difficulty and here is a promise. Would it be lawful to plead this promise in view of that difficulty?" But he says, "You cannot come to me with a question of that kind after I go away from here, but I will send you someone to whom you shall carry questions of that kind."

And the fact of the presence of the Holy Spirit suggests the other limitation. What is it? Anything that you ask of me that is Spirit-prompted, I will do. Is that true? Listen! I will read you from the Book itself, the eighth chapter of Romans: "Likewise the Spirit helpeth our infirmities, for we know not what we should pray for as we ought, but the Spirit himself maketh intercession for us with groanings which cannot be uttered. And he that searcheth the heart knoweth what is the mind of the Spirit, because he maketh intercession for the saints according to the will of God."

Now, if the Lord Jesus Christ were present and I saw a great big promise held out, and I wanted to utilize that promise of God to get rid of a certain difficulty, I would step right up to him and ask him to say if this was a pertinent case.

Suppose I ask this: "Will it be according to the will of God?" Just as when the mother of Zebedee's children came and said, "Lord, I want to ask you something. I have a petition to present to you." "Well, what is it?" "That my son James should have the place on thy right hand in thy kingdom." He frankly tells her that it is not a case in point—that there is nothing particular in the doing of this thing, in the partiality shown to James or John, that will in any way glorify the Father in the Son, and therefore that petition does not legitimately come under the promise. He was there to explain.

Now he is away and I want to offer a prayer under this promise. I want the prayer to be according to the will of God; that is to say, the prayer must correspond to the end that is to be accomplished by its granting. The prayer must be correlative with the merit upon which it is obtained. There must be harmony between what I ask for and the basis upon which I obtain it. And I don't know whether this prayer would fit that way or not and Jesus is not here for me to ask him, but the Holy Spirit is, and as I don't know what to pray for, nor how to pray for it, and I want my prayer to be according to the will of God, I go to the Holy Spirit.

What then is meant by the saying that the Holy Spirit maketh intercession for the saints? That does not mean that the Holy Spirit acts as a mediator between us and Jesus Christ, but it means this, that the Holy Spirit is on earth here, our Teacher, in the place of the Teacher that is gone, and that as that Teacher, when he was here, taught his disciples how to pray and what to pray for, the Spirit now takes his place as the other Paraclete and teaches us what to pray for and how to pray for it.

How does he do this? He does this by impressions made on the mind, made on the heart, impressions that you feel. Do you know what that means? I have heard some of you say, "I feel like my prayers do not go any higher than my head." And then I have heard you say at other times, "I felt as I prayed that my petition took hold of the throne of almighty

God." Why did you feel that way? There was One teaching you what to pray for and how to pray. There was an Instructor invisible to human sight and inaudible to human ears, but visible to faith, who had your heart under his omnipotent influence and who, with groanings unutterable, was directing your mind unto the things to be asked for that would be in accordance with the will of God.

Then perhaps somebody will say, "If this broad promise is limited that much it takes the whole of it away." It does take it all away if what you want with prayer is simply to gratify your lust; if it is simply to minister unto your carnal desires; if it is simply to add to your selfish accretions. Then it does you no good. There is no promise to you in it.

I close with this illustration: The disciples observed Jesus praying. There was something in the manner of his praying, and there was something in the confidence with which he prayed, and there was something in his face that showed that he received what he prayed for, all of which impressed them that such praying as they had learned of the Jews was no praying at all; that it was only saying a prayer; that it was not praying. Hence they come right up and say, "Lord, teach us to pray."

I took that lesson last night, the last thing that I did before I went to bed, and, getting down on my knees, I said, "O Holy Spirit, whose presence touches my very being, and whose presence is to guide me into all truth, just as Jesus would do if he were present here upon the earth, O Holy Spirit, impress upon my mind so that I will feel it and realize Christ's lesson on prayer." And I got up and took the lesson. You ask me to tell you how to pray. You ask me to teach you how to pray and what to pray for. Well, I will do it. Now listen: "Our Father." You are going to ask for some desirable thing. What is it? "Hallowed be thy name." Is that what you want? Yes, you want the name of God hallowed in reverence all over this earth; regarded not with profanity, but with reverence. Do you want that? Or do you want the Lord to give you a horse and buggy?

What else? Lord, teach me how to pray, "Father, thy kingdom come." Now, that will glorify the Father in the Son, and "Whatsoever ye ask in my name, I will do it." "Thy kingdom come." But "the kingdom of God does not consist in meat and drink, but of righteousness and peace and joy in the Holy Ghost." "Thy kingdom come to the Japanese, to the inhabitants of Thibet, to China, to Alaska, to Labrador, to the jungles of darkest Africa and to the slums of England. Thy kingdom come to every destitute mission field in Texas. Lord, I want, I desire, I thirst for, I pray for the coming of thy kingdom."

Well, let me see if you do: "If you love me, keep my commandments." "I have told you to carry my gospel to them. Are you doing it? Is the spirit of obedience on you when you ask that my kingdom come, and are you working to that end? If not, how dare you, you idle, stingy, narrow, contracted, shrivelled up, inert professors of religion, say 'Thy kingdom come'?"

What else? "Thy will be done on earth as it is in heaven." Is that what you want, or do you just want the Lord to give you a dozen new dresses, or do you want that your hand may be on the neck of your enemy, or do you want to ask the Lord that you and yours shall receive temporal greatness, and other people should become the foundation upon which that greatness stands? "Thy will be done upon earth as it is in heaven." That harmonizes with all the conditions.

Well, it is a pretty solemn thing to raise questions about the things that I desire. Is not the hallowing of God's name, is not the coming of God's kingdom, is not the doing of the will of God on earth as it is done in heaven, a very great desideratum? And didn't Christ die that these things might be done? Therefore there is a correspondence between the predicate of the prayer and the thing asked for. If these things be done, will they not glorify the Father in the Son? Therefore is there not correspondence? So I find out that I have

been desiring a great many things that related simply to myself
and that his promise did not touch.

Again, "Give me for today my daily bread." "But, Lord,
I have thought that I ought to have about six years' rations
laid up in advance." The Lord may enable you to do that,
but there is no use to pray for it. What you want to pray
for is your present need. You do not today need bread for
six years hence. "Sufficient for the day is the evil thereof."
You pray this: "Give me for today the bread for today."

What else? "Lead me not into temptation," but "if ye love
me keep my commandments." The commandment was, "Go
not in the way of sinners," for if you go in the way of sinners,
you are liable to fall into the errors of sinners. If you sit in
the seat of the scornful, if you walk in the counsel of the
ungodly, if you stand in the way of sinners, you are likely
to fall into temptation. But do I say, "Lord, lead me not into
temptation," while not keeping his commandments? Do I go
in the way of sinners, and put myself in danger, and thrust
myself right into the lion's jaw when there is no need for it,
and then do I say, "O Lord, don't let the lion bite me?"
"Deliver me from the evil one."

As the Lord said to the devil, "I will turn Job over to you,
but don't you touch his life." I will admit that the evil one
cannot blot your name out of the Lamb's book of life; but
if you do violate God's commandments, it may be necessary,
as it was necessary in the case of that Corinthian, to turn you
over to the buffetings of Satan for a while, that you may be
saved in the day of the Lord Jesus. But now I pray, "Deliver
me from the evil one. Lord, don't let him buffet me."

"Well, if you love me, keep my commandments, and I will
send you the Holy Spirit. The evil one shall not triumph
over you. Resist the devil and he will flee from you." But
have you resisted him? Or have you gone into his haunts, and
kept company with his people? Have you adopted their max-
ims of business? Have you loved card parties and theaters
more than you have loved prayer meetings? And have you

gone outside of the highway on which the Lord said no lion shall roar? And have you gone out here in the jungle which is the home of the lion, and now say, "O Lord, don't let the lion roar at me"?

I have tried, brethren, to set before you this promise. Oh, it is broad; it is mighty. It is broad enough to cover the whole earth. It is high enough to fill the whole earth, from its central cavity to the stars, with the glory of God. It is broad enough to fill the whole world, from the rivers to the ends of the earth, with the knowledge of God. It is broad enough to carry messages of life and salvation to all of the ignorant and the superstitious and the benighted and the perishing and the sick and the imprisoned. It is broad enough to carry comfort to every broken heart and to strike the chains off of every prisoner and to lift out from under the down-pressing foot of Satan the bursting hearts of his victims, and stand them up in the liberty of God, freed, and absolved from sin. It is broad enough for that, and for all of it.

Now, can we not claim it? Can we not lay aside the things that we selfishly want, and seek, according to the will of God, the outpouring of the power of our Lord Jesus Christ, who this day stands over us, holding omnipotence in his right hand, his left hand holding omnipresence, and from his heart going out infinite love, and saying, "I will do anything whatsoever; I will do it. Ask me to do it." Who can ask him? Who can present a petition in harmony with the end that will tend to glorify the Father in Jesus Christ? Let him, Spirit-prompted, offer this day the prayer of faith.

VI

"LORD, INCREASE OUR FAITH"

TEXT: *Lord, increase our faith.*—LUKE 17:5.

THE context embraces the first ten verses of this chapter. And it is well to note that in order of time, between the tenth verse of this chapter and the eleventh verse, there is a wide interval of many days and many wonderful events. There is no connection whatever as to time or thought between the first ten verses and the subsequent part of the chapter. But there is a direct connection between the first five verses and the second five.

This connection, when understood, suggests the occasion of the prayer of the disciples, "Lord, increase our faith." Hence our first question is, What occasioned that prayer? It is not the first time they offered that prayer, nor will it be the last. It is a common prayer of Christians, "Lord, increase our faith." But what led to this prayer this time? Evidently what he had just said about offenses, about stumbling. It is impossible but that occasions of stumbling will come. That is to say, as we are constituted, as matters now stand in the world, in view of the depravity of human nature, it is certain, it is unavoidable, that people fall into sin. You may be sure they will.

When the effects of the fall of man in Eden have been swept away and we live in a new earth and under a new heaven, it will not be impossible to live without sin, but it is impossible now. At the same time he says, "Woe unto that man by whom this occasion of stumbling comes. It were better that a millstone should be put about his neck and that he should be cast into the sea." Then he says, "If these little ones stumble, rebuke them, and on their repentance forgive, seventy times seven." Let there be no limit. Now, in view of these facts, the apostles say, "Lord, increase our faith."

If I live in a world like that, where on the right hand and on the left hand people are falling; where every path of life has its obstruction; where in addition to the natural obstacles there is an evil spirit disposed to increase the obstruction; where evil men are tempting God's people to fall into sin; if my whole pathway of life is beset by snares and traps and pitfalls, then "Lord, increase my faith."

If I must be circumspect in my own conduct as a preacher; if I must put a restraint upon my liberty; if in some cases I must not contend for my rights; if I must all the time consider other people as well as myself; if when I go to eat meat, knowing, though it has been offered to an idol, that the idol is nothing, and that that meat will not hurt me, yet as I am eating in the sight of some that are weaker, and they see me, and may put a construction upon my action that will cause them to fall into a sin—if I am to live under conditions of such watchfulness and such self-denial as that, "Lord, increase my faith."

And if an obligation rests upon me whenever I see a brother sin to faithfully rebuke him, to make an honest and faithful effort for his recovery, no matter how repugnant such a duty may be to me, no matter how timid my disposition may be, if the obligation of God is inexorable that I go and convince my brother of his sin and try to lead him back to God, then "O Lord, increase my faith."

And if, having convinced him one time and a second time, and seven times, and seventy times seven, and he manifests a disposition to stumble again, and the law over me is just as binding as it was at the start—"Go, convince him of his sin; go bring him back, and on his repentance truly forgive him again"—then, "Lord, increase my faith."

You see the connection, that we cannot hope as Christians to live in the path in which our Saviour commands us to walk, and to half-way discharge our duties here on this earth except by an all-pervasive, conquering principle of faith in God. Have faith in God!

This and the next thought are closely connected. He discerned in his disciples a spirit that needed to be corrected. He does not specify what the spirit is, but he leaves you to infer it from the lesson he teaches. See if you can so infer it, this fault he so kindly and delicately seeks to correct by this teaching: "Who is there of you, having a servant plowing or keeping sheep, that will say to him when he is come in from the field, Go straightway and sit down to meat, and will not rather say, Make ready wherewith I may sup, and gird thyself and serve me until I have eaten and drunken, and afterward thou shalt eat and drink. Would he thank the servant because he did the things that are commanded? Even so ye also when ye shall have done all the things that are commanded"—all the things, when you have been watchful over yourself lest you should lead a weaker brother into sin, when you have rebuked him in case he did sin, when you have convinced him of the sin that he committed and led him to repent of it, when upon his repentance you have forgiven him, when this forgiveness has been exercised seventy times seven, when you have done all that was commanded you, then say, "We are unprofitable servants. We have done that which it was our duty to do."

Now there was a fault in his disciples that he designed to correct by this teaching. What was it? And having such a fault, what was its relation to the prayer, "Lord, increase our faith"? It seems easy enough to find out that this fault was a feel of self-complacency, of self-satisfaction, of self-congratulation, when viewing the service we have performed. The temptation is persistent and insidious, and coming in a thousand Protean shapes assails us upon the right hand and on the left hand whenever we do anything that is right; a temptation that restrains our prayers when it makes us say, "See what a good man I am. Behold how excellent a Christian! See how self-denying I am; see how thoughtful about the weaknesses of others; see how I pay tithes of all that I possess! See how closely I follow in the footsteps of my Master! How could the Lord do without me? What would happen to this world if I should die? And oh, what a calamity to this community if I move to another community, and what a blessing upon that community if it shall gain me!" Do you see the spirit?

Pride dethroned an angel and dragged him down to chains of everlasting darkness. Pride was the condemnation of the devil, and we need continual watchfulness that it be not our condemnation. Now this spirit of pride was in the disciples. He is not here talking to the Pharisees. He is not talking to the unregenerate. He says, "Even so, ye also," ye disciples, my own people; there is in you, in every one of you, in the best of you, in the highest and noblest and humblest and truest of you, there is a continual danger of leaning to self-right-eousness, of feeling as if you had put God under an obligation, of feeling as if you were a very important steward, of feeling that he could not very well do without you.

But let me assure you, brethren, that if every one of us, in one moment, should instantly sink down to the depth of the ocean and leave no memento more lasting than the bursting bubbles that would rise, it would not in any sense interfere with the fulness and sufficiency of God. What can I confer upon him? If he were hungry would he ask me to feed him? From what resources can I gather a present to make unto the Lord? "Lord, increase my faith." In view of this internal enemy, this spirit of pride and self-complacency, that like a fly in the apothecary's ointment spoils its fragrance, "O Lord, increase my faith."

It seems incredible—the true things are always much more incredible than the fictitious—it seems incredible that in view of plain New Testament teaching any man ever should have supposed that he had done more than his duty; that having done more than his duty, by the amount of that excess he had created a fund of transferable grace and merit, what is called a work of supererogation, and that having thus in one case done more than he ought, this excess is entered to his

credit; there is a surplus; and that now if at some future
time he should fall short, he has only to check out of that
surplus and balance the books, and if he should keep on add-
ing to that surplus by doing more than he ought to do, and
then should die, leaving that surplus to the credit of the
church, and if there be a great many other good people like
him, and they leave their surplus to the church, then after
a while there will be a great fund of supererogation, so that
under the direction of the earthly head of the church, if some
man of the present day shall fall short, and he will do what the
church tells him to do, the church can check on that surplus
fund and patch out his work and make good what he had
omitted.

But, incredible as this appears, it has been taught by thousands, and millions have believed it. It is taught in the name
of Jesus Christ as if it were his doctrine, and how ready is
the carnal mind to receive it! Have you heard of the word
"indulgence"? Have you studied the history of the doctrine
of "indulgences" and marked its demoralizing influence on
human conduct? See the petitioner come to one credited
with the deposit of surplus good works. What would he have?
An "indulgence." Indulged in what? To omit right or commit wrong. To be absolved from duty or to obtain immunity
from wrong already done or wrong as yet only purposed.
Hear the petitioner: "I want to commit an offense, and before it is committed I want the account balanced by having
passed over to my credit the superfluous merit of God's people
that has been gathered up through the ages. For such gracious privilege I am willing to pay somewhat." Of course,
if there be such precious deposit of surplus excellence in the
hands of the church, and the church be disposed to sell this
valuable property, it will find a ready sale and create a bound-
less revenue. That was a wonderful scene in Germany when
Tetzel stood up and sold "indulgences"—sold privileges not
to do right, sold privileges to do wrong, sold them on the
ground that the church was the residuary legatee of all the

surplus good that had been done, and could check on that accumulated fund of excess of merit and balance accounts that were not even. Whenever you admire the dome of St. Peter's Cathedral in Rome, would it not be well to temper your admiration with the question: How much of this magnificence was paid for by Tetzel's sale of "indulgences"?

Now our Saviour knew human nature. He knew the tendencies of that nature. He anticipated such teaching. He knew the pride of the human heart, and therefore he said to these disciples, "When you have done everything that I command you to do, whatever it is, then speak to your soul and say, 'Unto God thou art an unprofitable servant.'" Though you work all day in the field plowing, or all day keeping sheep, thy night is God's as well as the day. When you return from the field work, though you then gird yourself and still serve your Lord through all the night watches until day comes again, even then thou shalt say, "I am an unprofitable servant. I have only done what it was my duty to do. I have simply fulfilled the law of my being. I cannot do more than right. I cannot accumulate a surplus fund of merit, even if I never sin, even if I always do right."

Consider another view of the case. It always made the apostle Paul ashamed to refer to what he had done, and he calls himself a fool every time he does it. He says, "Let me be a fool for your sake, when I recount what I have done and what I have suffered. Let me be a fool to talk about it. I have suffered a great deal. I have been whipped and stoned and imprisoned and left for dead. I have labored with these hands to support my necessities. I have labored more than all the other apostles. I have, night and day and with tears, devoted myself to the cause of Christ, here, there, everywhere; but who made me different from another? God. By his grace I am what I am, and not by my own merit. I was a sinner, a blasphemer, a persecutor without merit and without hope in the world, and God, out of infinite mercy, saved me and conferred a favor on me in letting me be his servant;

so that I have nothing of which to boast, nothing. And so I take up my crown, bright as it may be, and sparkling with stars as his grace may allow, and I lay it at the feet of my Redeemer and I say, 'Not unto me, not unto me, O Lord, but unto thy name, be honor and glory and power forever. I am only a sinner saved by grace.' " That is the true thought of the gospel.

Now in view of this natural disposition, this prevalent state of mind and heart to glory in one's self, this proneness to imagine a big balance in our favor, ought not every Christian to pray, "Lord, increase my faith—let me always have that kind of trust in God. Oh, keep back thy servant from presumptuous sins. Let them not have dominion over me. Let not the spirit of pride and self-complacency ever enter into my heart, and Lord, when I look up to heaven, let Jesus fill my vision and God be my only satisfying portion."

I put this question to my Bible class this morning as I put it to you. After reading, "Who is there of you, having a servant plowing or keeping sheep, that will say unto him when he is come in from the field, 'Come straightway and sit down to meat,' and will not rather say unto him, 'Make ready wherewith I may sup, and gird thyself and serve me until I have eaten and drunken, and afterward thou shalt eat and drink,' " the question was this: Is that part of the parable designed to teach God's treatment of his obedient servants? It seems to make on the mind a harsh impression concerning God. Is that part of the parable designed to teach God's attitude toward his faithful people? It is very clear that the parable is designed to teach what shall be our attitude of mind toward God; that we should say, "unprofitable servants"; that we should be willing to serve in the night though we had served in the day; that is clear. But is that part of it designed to represent God? And I answer, no, not at all. He would have a right to say that to us, but he does not say that.

In another connection we find his attitude. I read from the same Gospel of Luke, where the divine side of the thought is brought out, the twelfth chapter of Luke: "Let your loins be girded about and your lamps burning, and be ye yourselves like unto men looking for their lord when he shall return from the marriage feast, that when he cometh and knocketh they may straightway open unto him. Blessed are those servants whom the Lord when he cometh shall find watching. Verily I say unto you that he shall gird himself and make them sit down to meat and shall come and serve them." There is the divine side of it.

Now I cannot, on account of any Christian duty that I have performed, say to my Lord, "Inasmuch as I work hard for you all day you must come and wait on me at night." I cannot say that. I must say, "My night is thine as well as my day and I have no claim on thee. I brought nothing in my hands when I came to thee." But the Lord will say to me, "Sit thou down and I will gird myself, come and serve thee and wait upon thee."

It is well to notice the limitation of each parable and not to try to prove everything from one view of a subject. The plowing servant represents what our reverent and submissive thought Godward should ever be. The passage from Luke, the twelfth chapter, reveals God's gracious attitude toward us.

I will give you an object lesson on that. When the time came for our Lord to eat the last Passover, he sent two of his disciples to a certain place to make ready. Before going to eat the Passover, every Jew performed bodily ablutions, a complete bathing, but from that place of bathing to the house where they were to eat the Passover was an intervening distance, and in going over that, the feet would become dusty, having sandals only that did not cover the top of the feet, and hence when they got to the feast, he that was washed is clean already, needing only to wash his feet, but he did need to wash his feet. Now when they got to that upper chamber, somebody must make ready for performing the only ablution now necessary—the feet washing. But there is no servant here to do this, and the disciples had a dispute about it, those who esteemed themselves greatest being least willing to do a menial service. We can imagine how they discussed it. Peter, James, and John perhaps say, "It is evident from the fact that we have been singled out several times by our Lord that we are higher than the rest of you, and we cannot perform this menial service, and rather than to stoop we will sit down here and eat the Passover without having our feet washed." And so they did, and our Lord saw it, and he saw that spirit of pride, that devilish spirit of self-complacency, of self-exaltation, and without saying a word he got up and girded himself and took a basin and a towel and went around and commenced to wash their feet. "If I, your Lord and Master!" Oh, what a lesson it was! How it showed the incredible spirit of pride that there is in the human heart! How often the lesson of humility must be repeated! How often we need to pray, "Lord, increase my faith."

There remains for consideration one other thought: "If ye have faith as a grain of mustard seed ye may say unto this sycamine tree, be thou rooted up and be thou planted in the sea, and it will obey." As there was never an instance in the life of our Lord where on man's order a tree standing on the shore in an instant transferred itself to the bottom of the sea, and as there is no instance where our Lord or any of his disciples commanded a mountain to be moved over into the sea, and as these literal things are found only in the *Arabian Nights*, what did our Lord mean? What did he mean to teach? What was harder to do than to move a tree from land to sea? What was harder to do than by speaking a word to move a mountain into the ocean? There were obstacles in the way of right doing, obstacles that to unassisted human nature were as insuperable as the moving of a mountain by a simple dictum.

You are commanded as a Christian, every day of your life, to do things that are impossible. You are commanded to do things that no fallen human nature can do. Let us look at some of them. First, never so use your liberty so as to put an occasion of stumbling in the path of a weak brother; never fail to rebuke a brother when he sins; never fail to convince him that he has sinned and lead him back to penitence; never fail to forgive him fully and freely as God forgives, when he does repent; never permit the spirit of self-complacency and pride to rise up in your heart when you look back over your work or look at your sacrifices.

I tell you that I would sooner undertake the tunneling of Mount Cenis, and I would expect with more certainty, by a single word of mine, when Vesuvius and Aetna and Hecla and Popocatepetl are in full eruption—I would sooner expect to put out their fire by a word than to speak to my own proud heart with expectation of obedience: "Never be proud. Never lay flattering unction to yourself. Always do right." Give me the mountain.

And now, because these things are so hard to do, because, humanly speaking, they are impossible, because Omnipotence alone can do them, how can I make that Omnipotence mine? How can I use Omnipotence to put out volcanoes, to move mountains? How can I do it? By faith. God's power becomes my power. His omnific energy is laid under tribute, if only renouncing self, if only relying on Jesus, if only by faith I can look up to him and lean on him, by faith I can do all things. Then, "Lord, increase our faith."

Let us make an application of this. Our Saviour looked right into the eyes of eleven undowered, unlearned fishermen. They had none of the graces of cultivated society; they had no wealth; they had no army of friends. There was not a material resource upon the face of the earth upon which they could count. They had the dialect of the Galileans, so that their speech betrayed them. They had no trick of elocution or rhetoric. And he said to these men, "Go ye into all the world and preach the gospel to every creature. Go disciple all nations." "Lord, we cannot do it." "All power in heaven and on earth is given unto me; therefore, go, and I am with you alway, even unto the end of the world. Therefore, go." "How shall I know thou art with me? How shall I be conscious of thy presence? How shall I touch that power? How shall I do these impossible things?" "By faith." Then, "Lord, increase my faith."

And it is just that way in the performance of the simplest Christian duty, whatever it is. It is true that as you cultivate this faith, it, like a grain of mustard seed, begins to grow, until it is the greatest of all herbs, the consciousness of the divine presence increases, the sense of the undergirding of the divine arm all the time becomes stronger with you, and more and more you begin to feel that there is nothing too hard for God. The Spirit of the Lord is not straitened. God's ear is not deaf that he cannot hear. God can do anything whatsoever. Then, "Lord, increase my faith."

Oh, put me in touch with this divine power, and having faith in God, I will refrain from the exercise of my liberty if it makes my weak brother stumble. Having faith in God, if he does stumble, I will go to him and bring him back. Having faith in God, I will forgive him when he repents. Having faith in God, I will tear from my head all the fading laurels of earthly glory and I will put myself at the feet of my Redeemer, as a sinner, saved by his grace. Having faith in God, I will preach his simple gospel. Trusting in the Word of the Lord, "thus saith the Lord," eschewing all human means of gathering and holding men, turning away from them as from the plague, all cunning speech, all devices and tricks of elocution, and relying solely and wholly upon the simple gospel of Jesus Christ, I will go out preaching, and I will go out believing that the gospel is the power of God unto salvation of both Greeks and Jews.

I do not expect you to see what I show you now. I do not expect you to see it today. But you will see it. I say to you that under proper conditions of obedience to Jesus Christ, and under the prevalence of the gospel of Jesus Christ, which is just as certain to come here on this earth as the sun to shine, that this earth can produce and nurture two hundred and fifty billions of inhabitants. No plagues, no famines, no pestilences, no devils, no overshadowing by the woman in scarlet, false prophets dead and Babylon the great cast down, and the devil bound, and wars ended; no armies to take life; a world so thickly peopled and civilization advancing so fast that two hundred and fifty billions, instead of one billion, can occupy this planet, and there will be a thousand years of that kind —a thousand years of that peace. And in that thousand years there will be so many more people saved by the power of the gospel than have already existed on this earth, that the company of the lost, as compared with the company of the saved, "will not be more than the criminals in our jails and penitentiaries when compared to the citizens that are law-abiding in this country." It is possible with God. It is coming. The Jews will be converted. The Romanist power will be put down. The devil will be bound. A nation will be born to God in a day and the knowledge of the Lord will cover this earth as the waters cover the great deep. "Have faith in God." "Lord, increase our faith."

VII

SEEKING AND FINDING GOD'S FACE

TEXT: *If my people, who are called by my name, shall humble themselves, and pray and seek my face, and turn from their wicked ways; then will I hear from heaven, and will forgive their sins.*—2 CHRONICLES 7:14.

THIS is God's reply to Solomon's prayer at the dedication of the Temple. That prayer is remarkable for nothing more than four things. 1. It distinctly recognizes the fact that all of God's people will sin. 2. That chastisement will inevitably follow those sins. 3. It assumes that God makes adequate provisions for the forgiveness of those sins. 4. This provision is through the atoning sacrifices of the Temple. These statements involve a vast deal of doctrine. That you may the more clearly see the significance of this doctrine, I wish to enlarge the text by more elaborate restatement.

The first is that Solomon's prayer distinctly recognizes the fact that all of God's people will sin. Not that some of them will sin, and not that all of them may sin, but that every one of them will sin, and does sin. The scriptural proof of the correctness of this statement is ample. The prayer of Solomon is twice recorded in the Old Testament: in the eighth chapter of the first book of Kings, and in the sixth chapter of the second book of Chronicles, and in both of these records this precise language is used, "There is no man that sinneth not."

It is true that he repeatedly commences his statements with an "if." If a man sin against his neighbor; if he sin against God; if he sin by commission; if he sin by omission. But the "if" in this case does not imply doubt as to the fact of sin. It only implies probability as to the kind of sin, as to the form that the sin will take, but it never implies any doubt that the sin will take some form, whatever that may be. "For there is no man that sinneth not. Then hear thou in heaven and forgive."

[101]

It is reinforced by another declaration of Solomon in the book of Ecclesiastes, and the seventh chapter, where very properly he uses this language, "For there is not a just man upon the earth that liveth and doeth good and sinneth not." It is utterly impossible to make the language any broader or any stronger; and it harmonizes with the threefold declaration of the apostle John, who says this: "If we say that we have not sinned," past tense, "we make God a liar, and the truth is not in us." Second, "If we say that we have no sin," present tense, "we deceive ourselves and the truth is not in us." Third, "If any man sin we have an advocate with the Father, Jesus Christ the righteous."

It is also in harmony with that declaration of the apostle Paul in the fifteenth chapter of the letter to the Corinthians. I want to read it to you, commencing with the twenty-fourth verse: "Then cometh the end, when Jesus shall have delivered up the kingdom to God, even the Father; when he shall have put down all rule and all authority and power. For he must reign until he hath put all enemies under his feet. The last enemy that shall be destroyed is death, and when all things shall be subdued unto him, then shall the Son himself be subjected unto him that put all things under him, that God may be all in all."

This Scripture teaches that the mediatorial kingdom of Jesus Christ shall last as long as man needs a mediator. A mediator is a go-between—one who goes between two parties at issue—and as long as there is an atom of difference unsettled you need the mediator. Just as soon as the issue is completely settled, the office of mediator expires by limitation.

Now my point is that if any Christian should ever for one single moment reach a sinless state, in that moment he would not need a mediator. There would be no issues between him and God. He would not need an advocate, for there would be no case at law between him and the Supreme Judge. Whenever any man on this earth reaches a sinless state, he has passed beyond a mediatorial reign.

What I have read informs us that the mediatorial reign of Christ shall last until the last enemy shall be destroyed; and the last enemy that shall be destroyed is death; and until death is destroyed, the realm of the mediatorial kingdom remains; so no man this side of death ran claim that he has passed out of it.

Listen to this Scripture, Revelation 21:22. Here is a description of heaven, and of the universe after the mediatorial kingdom is ended. After Jesus Christ has turned over everything to the Father, the twenty-second verse says, in describing the heavenly city, "And I saw no temple therein." What does that mean? Solomon built a Temple and dedicated it by prayer, and in that prayer he assumes that all of God's people will sin, and that chastisement will come upon them for that sin, and prays that an adequate provision shall be made for those sins of his people, and the Temple was for that purpose.

As if he said, "O Lord, here is this temple. Here is an altar where sacrifices are offered to atone for sin. Here is a priesthood that takes up the blood of the sacrifice and carries it into the holy of holies, and intercedes for the sinner." But according to John, when the mediatorial kingdom is ended there will be no temple. No temple! No altar of sacrifice, and no need for one. No priest to offer blood, and no need for one; because there are no issues between God and man. The issues have been settled. The offices of the Temple, whether in its typical or antetypical nature, have been accomplished, and the last enemy has been destroyed, and they are at one with God, and at peace with God. But until you get to that state and condition when no temple is needed, no sacrifices, and no high priest, no man living can say, "I do not sin."

If this be true, then it settles some things very thoroughly. One is that God, by the sacrifice of a temple, whether typical or antetypical, God, by the ministry of a high priest, whether typical or antetypical, makes provision for the forgiveness of the sins of his people, and makes that provision on the ground that they will and do sin—every one of them. Hence they sin most heinously who say that they have no sin.

Now, let us look at the second point in Solomon's prayer; for unless you get this point clearly before you, you will not understand the text, which is God's answer to prayer. The second point is that when God's people sin, chastisement inevitably follows. It is according to an imperious law. No Christian can sin without being chastised.

Now listen to this Scripture. I read from the twelfth chapter of the letter to the Hebrews, fifth verse: "My son, despise not thou the chastening of the Lord, nor faint when thou art rebuked of him: for whom the Lord loveth he chasteneth." Find one professor of religion whom God does not chasten, and you find a professor of religion whom God does not love. "For whom the Lord loveth he chasteneth, and scourgeth every son whom he receiveth." "If ye endure chastening, God dealeth with you as with children, for what child is he whom the Father chasteneth not? But if ye be without chastisement, whereof all are partakers, then are ye bastards and not children. Furthermore, we have had fathers of our flesh, which corrected us, and we gave them reverence; shall we not much rather be in subjection unto the Father of spirits, and live? For they verily for a few days chastened us after their own pleasure; but he for our profit, that we might be partakers of his holiness."

See how this Scripture corroborates the first position: that God chasteneth every one of his children; that if there be one who claims to be his child and who is without chastisement, the absence of the chastisement disputes his claim to the filial relation, because all of his children are partakers of the chastisement. And he chastises to correct; he does not willingly inflict suffering. Then note that the sole object of the chastisement is to make the one chastised a partaker of holiness.

Here is a Christian who claims that he does not sin. I put this question to him: "Are you without chastisement?" "Yes." "Then you are no child of God, for he chasteneth everyone he receiveth." "Well, I am mistaken about that, I am not without chastisement." "Then you are chastised because of sin and for your profit, and the object of your chastisement is to make you a partaker of holiness. Why chastise the innocent?"

Let us get these points now, right clearly fixed in our minds: That the power of Solomon's prayer is based upon three things. 1. That God's own people, after they become his people, every one of them, without any exception, will sin and do sin. 2. That the chastisement of God comes as an inevitable consequence of that sin. 3. A petition that God may make adequate provision for the forgiveness of such sins. And mark you, the petition is that the provision be connected with the temple, with the sacrifice of blood, with the intercession of the high priest, and he particularly says this, "Lord, let thy name be here, and thine eyes here, and thine ears here, and thy power here." And when God answers that prayer he answers it just exactly that way. He says, "My name shall be there, and mine eyes shall be there, and mine ears shall be there, and my heart shall be there."

So whenever any one of God's people anywhere commits a sin, the way to get rid of that sin may be easily understood, and that there may be no delay about it, the very first step that he takes toward seeking remission, God sees it. The very first trembling word, petitioning for forgiveness, God hears it. His ears are there, and his eyes are there. The very first step toward the Father, the heart of God goes out to meet him. "My heart shall be there."

Now we are prepared to make two statements: that whoever claims to be sinless has passed beyond the mediatorial kingdom of Jesus Christ, has passed beyond the realm of chastisement, if what he says is true. But as the mediatorial kingdom of Jesus Christ lasts until the last enemy shall be destroyed, which is death, and such state where there is no temple, is after the end of the mediatorial kingdom; therefore no man on earth and in time is sinless.

This leads up to the theme: plain directions to Christians who are out of the way, telling them how to get back in the way. What are those directions? Now, let us repeat the text: "My people who are called by my name shall humble themselves"—(direction 1); "and pray"—(direction 2); "and seek my face"—(direction 3); "and turn from their sins"—(direction 4); "then will I forgive them."

There cannot possibly be a subject of greater practical interest to Christian people than this subject. Are you a Christian? Then if the position stated is correct, you are all today out of the way—how far out of the way, I do not know, nor do you. That you are not all equally far out of the way is self-evident; but that every one of you is somewhat out of the way follows from the proposition already established. Now if you are to any extent out of the way, it is all-important, co-extensive with the degree of your departure from God, that you get back in the way. Get back there for peace. Get back there for power. Get back there for strength. And getting back there is a revival.

How important it is to people who are out of the way to have very simple, very plain directions showing how to get back in the way, to know the direction, to know just what to do. In simple language, what am I to do to get back in the way? Now here is God's answer to it. What is the first thing? "Humble myself." As soon as we come to this first direction, we are instantly put upon the definition of humility. How are you to know? If you are to humble yourself, you must know.

What is humility? Listen to this sentence: "God resisteth the proud but giveth grace to the humble." Here stand two things over against each other and define each other. Humility then is the antipode of pride; just as light is the opposite to darkness, and truth is the opposite to error. So that when we come to define humility, we may not think that we have gotten to the true conception of it, so long as the ground occupied by our definition does not stand squarely opposite to the ground occupied by pride.

Let us get a little nearer the etymology of the word. It is from "humus." Humus means "ground." The idea derived from its etymology clings to it always, and we have never gotten a correct definition of humility, when we separate it from its etymological conception—the ground. Humus—the ground—humility. So that in this definition must be the conception of putting one's self low down on the ground, next to the ground. To humble one's self then is not to be lifted up, which is pride, but to put one's self down on the ground.

Let us get it a little more closely. If I were trying to analyze humility, I would state it somewhat negatively this way: A humble man does not over-rate himself, does not put himself up too high. On this point hear Paul in the twelfth chapter of the letter to the Romans: "For I say, through the grace given unto me, to every man that is among you, not to think of himself more highly than he ought to think; but to think soberly according as God hath dealt to every man the measure of faith." Whoever then over-rates himself is not humble. Whoever thinks too highly of himself is not humble.

Then he must not over-rate his ability. The Scripture says, "Let not him that putteth on the harness boast as he that putteth it off." So when you find a man speaking of something which is to be accomplished, an untried experiment, using great swelling words of vanity, over-rating his abilities, priding himself upon his power, that man is not an humble man.

Let us proceed in the analysis. When he over-rates his possessions he is not humble. Hear the Scripture again: "And because thou sayest, I am rich, and increased with goods, and have need of nothing, and knoweth not that thou art wretched, and miserable, and poor, and blind, and naked." And now, whenever a man over-rates his possessions, he under-rates his needs correspondingly. If he says, "I am rich, I therefore need nothing," but if it be true that he is blind, and poor, and miserable, and naked, in order for him to get a conception of his need, he must put himself down where he belongs. Get down on the ground. Get down! Get down lower! Lower yet! Get down until you touch the ground. Humus—humility.

Now it is of vast importance that you notice another point in analyzing humility. It is discovered by what we glory in. You need not ask a man what he glories in. But watch him and you will see what he glories in. If he glories in himself, in his power, in his possessions, in his achievements, if you can see complacency stealing over him, you may know that he isn't humble. But if he glories in the Lord, that is different: "I am well; I glory in him that made me well. I am clean; I glory in him whose blood cleansed me. I am rich; I glory in him who became poor that I might be made rich; by the grace of God I am what I am."

Now, in that sort of way you may get at the true conception of humility. But, mark you: If humility is analyzed by looking at one's rating of himself or his, whether he over-rates or under-rates, do you know that when you use that word "rate," you necessarily imply a standard? Where there is no standard, there can be no rate. Suppose I were to measure that goblet by itself. If I measure it by itself, it is utterly impossible to detect any defect in it, because nothing measured by itself will reveal defects. If I measure it by another goblet, also imperfect, I never get at a correct result. There must be some fixed and perfect standard by which both are to be measured, and so when a man begins to rate himself in order to determine whether he is humble, he must not measure himself by himself, nor must he measure himself by some other imperfect being, but he must measure himself by the true standard, which is God. And whenever any man, however proud or conceited, however supercilious to superiors or contemptuous to inferiors, though his complacency be as big and as wide as the ocean, can be led to measure himself by the standard, God, you will see him get down on the ground.

Consider Job, how he did, maintaining his integrity and defying his friends when they disputed with him. But when God speaks to him out of the whirlwind, then Job says, "I abhor myself and repent in dust and ashes." He got down. He struck the ground that time. Humus. Humility. That right reading of one's self comes only when we are near to infinite holiness and purity.

Isaiah is another example. He was a sinful man and not much disturbed about it, but when he saw the Lord, whose train filled the temple, he fell as if he was shot. He struck the ground, and striking it, said, "I put my lips in the dust. I am a man of unclean lips and I dwell among people of unclean lips, and I have seen the Lord of hosts." So we arrive at the conception of humility. Rate by the Standard, which is God; putting yourself right down on the ground; that is humility.

An understanding of the next point is also essential. It would seem unnecessary to discuss it if there were not so many delusions. Humility is not a matter of words and dress. Did you ever read in Dickens' *David Copperfield* of Uriah Heep? Uriah and his mother? In words and dress they were the humblest people in England. They got down to the lowest place they could find, so far as words go, but at heart they were consumed with pride and envy.

In Shakespeare's *Julius Caesar*, look at Mark Antony, apologizing for his very existence. See how humble he stands there. Oh! He only comes to bury Caesar, not to praise him —to honor Brutus, not to censure him. Brutus is an honorable man. These all are honorable men. Oh, how humble! And yet in those words of humility he stirs up the very stones to mutiny. And Shakespeare's genius failed in only one thing. He should have represented Mark Antony standing with solemn face over the dead body of Brutus, and distributing certificates that he had always said that Brutus was an honorable man. It is not a matter of words.

Take another case. There stands Amasa and here comes Joab. Now watch. See him as he comes. What does he say to Amasa? "My brother Amasa, art thou in health, my brother?" and stabs him under the fifth rib. This necessitates a question: Did the words, "My brother, art thou in health, my brother," keep that deed from being assassination?

Look again: Yonder in a garden is Jesus, and his enemies are coming. See Judas leading them and hear him: "Hail, Master," as he kisses him. Did the "Hail, Master," and did the kiss prevent that act from being treachery? Did not Jesus pass upon it when he said, "Judas, betrayest thou the Son of man with a kiss?" Hear prophecy foretell that transaction: "For it was not an enemy that reproached me; then I could have borne it; neither was it he that hated me that did magnify himself against me; then I would have hid myself from him. But it was thou, a man mine equal, my guide, and my acquaintance. We took sweet counsel together and walked unto the house of God in company." The words of his mouth were sweeter than honey and smoother than butter, but war was in his heart. His words were softer than oil.

Do be impressed that humility is not a matter of words. What is it then? Listen to the Scripture: "Serving the Lord with all humility of mind and heart." Nor is it a matter of dress. A man is not humble because he is poorly dressed. He may be as proud as the devil and yet be in rags. Or he may be dressed in broadcloth and yet be humble. Humility is internal.

We started with the proposition that all God's people will sin. Every one of them does, and you know you do. Then followed the second proposition: That after such sin God will certainly chastise you. There is no escape from it; and the third proposition, that God has made adequate provision for the forgiveness of such sins.

Then comes this text with directions clear and simple. They tell you just what to do. Get back into the way of a Christian, and the first direction is to humble yourself. Now, that is the first. And let me tell you there is a relation between the first direction and the second, an essential and vital relation. I do mean to say that you cannot take the second step first, but must take the first step in order to the second. What is the first? Humble thyself. Second? Pray. For if a man says, "I am rich, I need nothing," how can he ask God for anything? How can he? But if humility has put him on the ground, and he realizes in his heart, "I have sinned; I am sick; I am needy; I am wretched," those needs suggest the petition; that first, and therefore the second direction, pray, pray. Whatever the need, wherever the crisis—pray.

Indulge me in a personal reference explaining how to pray. In the great Convention at Marshall one day when everybody else had left the room, I locked the door and humbled myself. In my spirit I got right down on the ground—low down in the dust. And there I felt a need, and that need was transmuted into a prayer to Jesus, and never in my life have I known a prayer to be answered sooner and more certain than that prayer was. There was a crisis in denominational affairs in which I was keenly interested. So much so I distrusted myself. I feared that I might prescribe to the Almighty in my prayers. So, renouncing self utterly, I prayed in agony and tears that the result might be just what the Lord wanted, even if it crucified all my desires. A sweet and holy calm filled my heart. All doubt of the result and all anxiety about it left me completely.

Now you can be revived. I know what you want. I know that your church wants a revival of religion. Surely that is what you want. I am giving you the directions how to get it. First, humble thyself. See the Pharisee and the Publican: "God, I thank thee that I am not as other men are." Look at the other: "God, be merciful to me a sinner." There they stand over against each other in awful contrast. Pride, the mountain; humility, the sweet valley. Humble thyself. That Pharisee felt no need. But the Publican, low down in humility, prayed for mercy. How sweet, and I never knew one so humbling himself to fail to reach the throne of God and fail to get an answer.

Are you despairing because so far off today? Your distance from God makes no difference. What is distance to

Omnipresence? If you will get down—get down on the ground
—get down in your spirit, in your mind, in your heart, and
then pray, I will know you are coming home. What, without
further amplifications, are the directions? "Humble yourself.
Pray. Seek my face." When a man has committed a sin, he
does not want to see the one against whom he sinned. When
Adam sinned in the garden, he hid when he heard God coming, and it is natural for the offender to skulk out of the way
of the offended. But the direction of God to the offender says
imperatively: "Seek my face." Don't run from God. You
never will settle it by going away. You only add to the distance. Turn toward him and keep on going until you meet him.

Do look at that prodigal son and see the whole thing illustrated: "And when he came to himself"; "I will seek his
face." Just look at it. But where do you find God's face?
Beyond the mediatorial kingdom; when you are sinless seek
God's face directly. There will be no go-between, no mediator between you and God. In the New Jerusalem, where is
no temple, and no sacrifice, seek God's face directly. But you
cannot seek the Father directly now, because you are a sinner.
If you so seek his face, you will die. How then can I? You
must seek his face in the Lord Jesus Christ. "I and the Father
are one." "Have I been so long time with you, and yet hast
thou not known me, Philip? He that hath seen me hath seen
the Father." Now when you want to see his face, see it in
Christ. There is the Sacrifice, and the Substitute. Seek his
face in Jesus.

Now the last thing. What has made this issue between you
and God? I mean after you became a Christian. Sin. What,
then, now concerns you? Get forgiveness for that sin. But
can you conceive of being forgiven for it, and yet retain it?
"Can a man be pardoned and retain the offense?" Shall you
ask God to put you back in the way by forgiving your sin, and
put your sin back there with you? That would be putting you
out of the way. But you want to get back. You say you do,

and you want to humble yourself, and you want to seek God's face.

Then, my brother, what are you to do with the things that made the issue? Meet that squarely. Here is a sin that you have committed. God's Word says turn from it. Turn away from it. Let him that stole steal no more. Let him that got drunk get drunk no more. Shall a man with maudlin speech ask God's forgiveness for drunkenness? But you may rejoice that my whole argument is based on the proposition that a man cannot be perfectly sinless. That is true. How do we evade that difficulty? You must turn away from your sin with your heart. In your heart you must hate it. You must turn away from it by putting it on Christ, and that you do by faith.

You say, "Lord, here is an offense of mine. I committed it after my conversion. But now, O Lord, in my heart I loathe it. I turn away from it. I know I am liable again to commit the same offense, but I hate it. I serve God, and I turn away from it, and I take the offense and I lay it right over on the Substitute, Jesus Christ. Now I can turn away from it, can't I?" How do I show that I have turned away from it? Why, if I have put the offense on Jesus Christ, it doesn't crush me. I know that a thing cannot be at two places at the same time, and if it is on him, I am free. I put it upon Jesus by faith. I put it on Jesus and all that offense is gone. In my heart I hate it.

Now, that is what God means by turning away from sin. He does not mean that you ever will in this life become sinless, for then we would need no temple, no priest, no sacrifice. But let us suppose that you have been of the opinion that you are sinless. Now, I ask you to look at this logically. If yesterday you reached the sinless point, then you did not need the High Priest to intercede for you. But the theory is that we need a High Priest without beginning of days or ending of years, who is able to intercede for us. And there is no question that one who claims to be sinless denies the eternal priesthood, denies the presence of the mediatorial kingdom, denies that the city without a temple is beyond the resurrection and the judgment.

Let us all, then, this day, seek God's face in Jesus Christ. Your pastor would lead you. I get down in the dust with you. Let every one of us obey the fourth direction: Humble thyself. Get down. Get down in your spirit. "Blessed are the poor in spirit." Blessed are they. Get down to the ground. Humus. Brother, get down today. O humble thyself before God! Get low down. When down, pray: "God, be merciful to me, a sinner." Then seek God's face in Christ, in Jesus. Pray, and then in your heart turn away from sin. Turn from it, and leave it on Jesus. Leave it there by faith, and walk away from it in the joy of reconciliation.

Lord, we put on our lips, because it comes from our hearts, the prayer of Daniel: "We have sinned and committed iniquity, and have done wickedly and have rebelled, even by departing from thy precepts and from thy judgments. O Lord, righteousness belongeth unto thee; to the Lord our God belong mercies and forgiveness; now, therefore, O our God, hear the prayer of thy servant; O Lord, hear!"

VIII

THE FEAR OF MAN A SNARE

TEXT: *Not that which entereth into the mouth defileth the man; but that which proceedeth out of the mouth, this defileth the man. Then came the disciples and said unto him, Knowest thou that the Pharisees were offended, after they heard this saying? But he answered and said, Every plant, which my heavenly Father hath not planted, shall be rooted up. Let them alone: they be blind leaders of the blind. And if the blind lead the blind, both shall fall into the ditch.*—MATTHEW 15:11-14.

OUR relation to God is the first of all relations in importance. Its obligations are paramount. The fear of man's judgment—the desire to please men—becomes a snare when it leads us to put the creature above the Creator. It is a convincing evidence of depravity, a cogent proof of flabbiness in moral fiber when we become unduly sensitive to public opinion. It reveals that we have no fixed, no supreme standard of right and wrong. Washington Irving tells us in Knickerbocker's *New York* that the Dutch governor's servant climbed upon the roof at the mansion and set the weathercock every morning according to his best judgment of the way the wind was blowing, and then all the people set their weathercocks by the governor's, so all the vanes in the city arbitrarily pointed for that day, regardless of higher law. Now are many of us better than the simple Dutch in Irving's satire? Not "What is right according to divine law," do we ask, but, "What is the fashion, what says society, what do our leading people say?"

Educated in this man-fearing, man-pleasing spirit, many group up so exceedingly sensitive, so apprehensive of wounding others that you might not miss it far to say that their idea of the "chief end of man" is not to offend men. Their theory is about this: the main thing, the sum of human duty, is so

to pass through life as not to offend anybody or combat any·
thing. Converted into precept: never take a position that will
make anybody mad, never avow an offensive doctrine, repress
your individuality, rub off salient angles, become round, and
when round, become soft. If others make sharp issues which
invade your neutrality, be noncommittal, trim, straddle, com-
pliment both sides, stick to generalizations, such as, "There are
good and bad in all parties and religions," or "It matters little
what one believes, so he lives right." If these rude disturbers
of your peace insist on alignment, whisper to them aside that
you admire their courage, wish you could imitate it, and only
wait a favorable opportunity to come out openly, but owing
to cruel circumstances over which you have no control, you
cannot just now afford to have opinions, much less express
them.

Our context shows that the disciples of our Lord were not
free from this servile spirit. Two antagonistic, aggressive, and
irreconcilable forces had met in conflict—Phariseeism and the
gospel of Jesus. The issue came on the question: "What is
sin?" The insuperable obstacle in the way of reconciliation
was a difference in the standards defining sin, the word of
God versus human tradition. The Pharisees held to a mass
of traditions not then written, but since embodied in the Talmud. This mass had accumulated in three ways. First, many
alleged teachings of Moses never reduced to writing but trans-
mitted orally from father to son. Second, the various decisions
of Jewish courts construing, under appeals to their tribunals,
the written text. Third, the comment on the text by various
learned rabbis. These traditions became the unwritten law.
Of course the practical question was inevitable: Which standard is paramount in case of conflict, the written or unwritten
law? On this point the Talmud of Jerusalem says, "The words
of the scribes are more lovely than the words of the law: for
the words of the law are weighty and light, but the words of
the scribes are all weighty." Elsewhere it declares that it is
a greater crime to "transgress the words of the school of

Hillel" than the law. And again: "My son, attend to the words of the scribes, more than to the words of the law." (Quoted from Broadus on Matthew.)

This same Pharisaic exaltation of tradition over God's written Word characterizes the papacy today and, coloring all its theological teaching, gives rise to as curious cases of conscience on the nature of sin as the case of our context. To offend this spirit is now as dangerous as it was in the days of Jesus Christ. And there is now the same jelly-fish subserviency to human judgment, the same men-fearing and men-pleasing spirit that prompted the disciples to say, "Knowest thou that the Pharisees were offended at this saying?"

From the introductory Scriptures read, you see the issue: "Why do thy disciples transgress the traditions of the elders? For they wash not their hands when they eat." Very sternly, in no honeyed words, our Lord met the issue. Every point of his counter-accusation is terrible: "According to your own prophets ye are hypocrites; ye substitute lip service for heart service; ye make void the law of God by your traditions; ye blot out the fifth commandment by a pretended vow. Changing the law standard ye change the nature of sin, making that to be sin which is no sin, and making that to be righteousness which is sin."

Then followed his great parable, which in one terse sentence digs up all Phariseeism by the roots, "Hear and understand: Not that which entereth into the mouth defileth the man; but that which proceedeth out of the mouth, this defileth the man." Which parable he thus interprets: "Perceive ye not, that whatsoever goeth into the mouth passeth into the belly, and is cast out into the draught? But the things which proceed out of the mouth come forth out of the heart; and they defile the man. For out of the heart come forth evil thoughts, murders, adulteries, fornications, thefts, false witness, railings; these are the things which defile the man: but to eat with unwashen hands defileth not the man."

The proverb, "Cleanliness is next to Godliness," will serve for an advertisement of Pear's soap, but it is far from being scriptural. Those who receive the high wages of unrighteousness are usually externally clean and well dressed, while many of the purest in heart are in homely dress and grimed with toil. It is an awful sin to count dirt as sin.

But our concern today is with the weakness of the disciples. "Lord, were you not too harsh in that statement; were you not rude, impolite, inconsiderate of the feelings of others? Lord, did you know that you had offended the Pharisees? They constitute an influential class, indeed are the chief people of our nation. They sit in Moses' seat. They are leaders in society and give tone to fashion. Their cue is the popular cry. Now, was it expedient to offend these people? In view of their standing, would it not have been better to soften the asperities of your doctrine and accommodate it to the ruling classes? Is there not danger of being righteous over-much?"

Such is the fair import of their rebuke. Why cannot all men see that it is impossible to reconcile these two oppositions, first, human tradition versus God's Word; second, ceremonial services versus moral and spiritual duties? Men are prone to make old religious usage an authority and to take so much more interest in it than in express commands of God, that they practically alter the divine law to harmonize with their custom. Fallen human nature so tends to be more interested in the external than in the moral and spiritual that we not infrequently witness the disgrace of neglecting the highest and holiest commands of God for the sake of mere human usages.

How, then, could our Lord be faithful to himself and his mission and not give offense? To require only lip service would not offend man, but would offend God. To require heart service would please God but offend man. "Honor thy father and thy mother" is not only a divine law, but is founded in nature, arising from the filial relation. That relation entails mutual obligations on parent and child which may not be nullified. The parent must cherish the child in helpless infancy and safely direct his youth. The child must obey the parent in all things lawful and cherish father and mother in their helpless old age. It would seem that our Lord might without offense to any insist on compliance with such obligations. But not so. Tradition had freed the child from the law of God. The liberty conferred by tradition exempted the child from conformity to both natural and revealed law. "Lord, if you insist on that antiquated fifth commandment you will offend the Pharisees."

Mark the reply of Jesus: "Every plant which my heavenly Father hath not planted shall be rooted up." Here the plant means doctrine. Spare your needless anxiety, brother. Let not your heart fail you for fear of things which seem to impend. Have faith in God. Take no counsel of your fears. Say not within yourselves: "See how error is spreading! See how false doctrines obtain credence! See how the advocates of evil are multiplying!" Be easy in your minds. Possess your souls in patience. What is contrary to God will be rooted up. Not now perhaps, but ultimately surely. Remember the parable of the tares and of the net. The Lord cometh.

What next says our Lord? "Let them alone." But this means what? Can it mean that no effort must be put forth to combat error? If it means that, Jesus was violating his own precept. Very faithfully did he expose error. Even unto death he witnessed against sin. What then does he mean by saying, "Let them alone"? It was a rebuke to the anxiety of the disciples. They were busying themselves with concern about offending errorists. His words are equivalent to these: "Turn loose your anxieties about these people. Let them alone in the matter of your needless concern." Do you suppose, my brethren, that such doctrines as Jesus preached could slip along in the world as smoothly as flowing oil? Make no noise? Create no disturbance? Stir up no excitement? Give no offense? Awaken no hostility? Did he come to send peace on earth? I tell you a sword rather. His gospel must at times

make a man's foes those of his own household, pitting father
against son and mother against daughter.

And why? Because our duty to God is paramount. It
takes precedence of human relations. As the world is evil, it
turns the world upside down. It must overturn and overturn.
It must slay before giving life. It must drain the moral Oke-
fenokee swamps, cut down its jungles, let in the light, however
much its slimy denizens may squirm, or however dolefully its
owls may hoot. O ye timid, ye fearful ones, ye shrinking and
sensitive ones, so anxious to court the world and conciliate
its favor, hear ye the word of the Lord: "If any man love
the world, the love of the Father is not in him. The friendship
of the world is enmity with God. For all that is in the world,
the lust of the flesh, and the lust of the eyes, and the pride of
life, is not of the Father, but is of the world. And the world
passeth away and the lust thereof; but he that doeth the will
of God abideth forever."

Have you yet to learn, my brethren, that to preach a gospel
which unveils all hidden things of dishonesty, that shines into
the secret chambers of thought, exposing every slimy thing,
that requires crucifixion of self and supreme love to God and
man—do you think that gospel contravening all depravity and
thwarting all selfishness can fail to excite undying hatred and
war just in proportion to its power? Does human nature
change with lapse of time? Does the veneer of so-called
modern civilization never crack its surface, revealing the grin-
ning, scowling, vicious brutality within?

Here is an example: There sits my brother pastor from
the distant border city of El Paso. He is announced to preach
tonight. A few weeks ago it was hardly safe for him to walk
the streets of El Paso in the daytime. Why? Can you not
anticipate me? Well, our pugilistic friend, Dan Stuart, had
virtual possession of El Paso, trying to bring off a prize fight
across the New Mexico border two miles away. But this
preacher and two others wired Congress of the impending fact
and that the territorial governor was powerless because there

was no law to forbid the brutalizing exhibition. Congress responded by instant legislation. Whereupon the howl: "These three preachers have cost El Paso $50,000!" Did you know, my brother, that you offended people by that telegram? Could you not have learned from Paul's example at Ephesus not to offend trade? Have you forgotten Demetrius and his slogan, "By this craft we have our wealth"? Why did you not prophesy smooth things?

Find another application in your Sunday school lesson today. Peter's rebuke of our Lord because he had showed plainly the imperious necessity of his vicarious passion. The devil first suggested, in the temptation, a Messiahship that would win the sovereignty of the world, if only Jesus would not disturb Satan and leave out the atonement. How clearly does our Lord point out the great danger and its antidote. What danger? The danger of being ashamed of Jesus. Ashamed of him at heart? No. Ashamed of him before the world, before men, on the streets, in business, in the secular papers. Ashamed to come out on the Lord's side, challenging attention of men, angels and devils to your confession: "Here I stand. I can do no other. I am a follower of Jesus. I avow it. My only shame is my unworthiness. My faults mar my profession. I wish I were better. But even such as I am, I am for Jesus now and forevermore."

Our Lord, in your very lesson today, shows how impossible it is to touch religion lightly. Hear his words: "If any man will come after me, let him deny himself, and take up his cross, and follow me. For whosoever will save his life shall lose it; and whosoever will lose his life for my sake and the gospel's shall save it. For what shall it profit a man if he shall gain the whole world, and lose his own life? Or what shall a man give in exchange for his soul?"

You cannot partially acknowledge his sovereignty. There is no room for compromise. You may not hold with him in some things and against him in others. He scouts the miserable subterfuge. It is for or against. There is no middle ground, no "free zone" as broad as the edge of a razor. Ye that try to go in two opposite directions, on you come shame, discomfiture, and irreparable disaster. "What will it profit a man, if he gain the whole world and lose his own soul?"

Allow me to find a climax in the example of the most illustrious contemporary of our Lord. You recall the title of Mrs. Evans' great work of fiction, *At the Mercy of Tiberius,* suggested by a statue of the third Caesar. Tiberius was now Roman emperor while Jesus speaks these words. He had the sovereignty of all the world.

Who was Tiberius? A distinguished Roman, educated by Augustus, a brilliant general, who obtained four triumphs. He it was that quelled insurrection in that very Armenia, whose woes now excite universal compassion. He put Tigranes on the Armenian throne, extorted from the Parthians the eagles lost by Crassus, snatched victory from the Barbarians on the Raetian Alps, overwhelmed by many disastrous defeats the indomitable Germans, adopted as the son of Augustus by whom he was compelled to divorce a wife he loved, to marry the shamefully dissolute daughter of the Emperor, and after the death of Augustus he was raised to the imperial throne.

What a man! How cold and hard! When the city of Troas presumed by embassy to offer condolence for the death of his son, his brutal, sarcastic response was that he condoled with Troy on the death of her illustrious citizen, Hector! Finally, weary with empire and triumph, he is now in the island of Capri, given over to most hellish orgies and beastly sensualities. He has all the world. About the time Jesus is speaking the foregoing words, Tiberius is trying to reply to certain interrogatories of his obsequious senate. Tacitus preserves the letter. Hear this letter from the man who owns the world: "What to write to you or how to write, I know not; and what not to write at this time, may all the gods and goddesses torment me more than I daily feel that I am suffering, if I do know." What awful disclosure is here! First, inexpressible pain. Second, pain every day. Third, hopeless ignorance, in the depths of agnosticism: "I know not what to write nor what not to write."

When a young man, he was as straight as Apollo, handsome as Adonis and as majestic as Mars. But now his face is so blotched with the signal flags of debauchery he is ashamed to be seen. His once stalwart form is now like Nebuchadnezzar's, so bowed by excess he moves almost on all fours like a beast. Four years after Christ was crucified, this man also died. And how? In a village not far from Rome he had hidden his marred form and visage, guarded from intrusive inspection by a cordon of imperial troops. As if to say, "Let no man see my blotched face. Let no prurient curiosity witness the painful movements of my bowed form." Courtesan and courtier left him, while the Roman mob, like a growling tiger, kept shouting, "To the Tiber with Tiberius." Becoming unconscious, he was gladly reported dead and a successor announced. Reviving, slaves smothered him under old clothes. What did it profit the man to gain the whole world and lose himself?

Thou hesitating, compromising soul, thou fool, shutting thine eyes to the alternative of Jesus and daring to touch religion lightly, draw near and look at Tiberius. Do come and look! He had all the world. But O look at the blotched face of Tiberius! Look, man, at the bent form of Tiberius! Touch the flickering pulse of Tiberius! Read the anguish and horror in the eyes of Tiberius! Contemplate the ignorance of Tiberius! Why shakes yonder pile of old clothes? Lift them and behold the hideous, gasping, smothering Tiberius! Catechize him in the interval of dying groans. Bend over him and whisper, "O Tiberius, one question before you pass away: What does it profit a man to gain the whole world and lose his own soul?" Think you he heard? Try it in this form: "O Tiberius, what now would you give in exchange for your soul?" O my brethren, compare. Hear Paul about to die under a murderous sentence of the successor of Tiberius: "For I am already being offered and the time of my departure is come. I have fought the good fight, I have finished my course" (2 Tim. 4:6-8).

Do you not hear the echo of Balaam's voice: "Let me die the death of the righteous, and let my last end be like his"? (Numbers 23:10.) But what eternal horrors hang around the death of the lost! His lamp is put out! Eternal night shrouds him in outer darkness! O when you think of the latter end of the wicked, very lovingly, very tenderly, very kindly, and with infinite patience bear with their faults. Divest yourself of every shred of animosity. Kindle in your hearts a desire that Niagara outpoured on it cannot quench—a desire that they may be saved. Pray for them. Speak to them. Plead with them. Bear with them. Hold up before them Jesus Christ as their only hope. Stop not to be anxious lest some be offended. Preach the Word. Preach it in tears. Preach it in faith. Preach it in hope. Preach it in the power of the Holy Ghost. Father, Father in heaven, pour out on this church thy Holy Spirit! Revive us, O Spirit of Life, breathe, breathe on the valley of dry bones, and make an army rise up!

THE GHASTLY TRAGEDY OF SAUL

Text: *I forced myself.*—1 Samuel 12:12.

I READ a long time ago a little story of this kind: There were two princes, the elder one the rightful heir to the throne and well deserving of that position. The younger had evil affections. He was envious, jealous and ambitious, selfish and unworthy to rule. He had no positive qualification for the high position which he desired to occupy, but he coveted it, and so, taking advantage on a certain occasion of his elder brother, he bound him, put out his eyes, locked him up and reported that he was dead. When visitors came, he would put a gag in his brother's mouth so that he could not cry out. And when he heard that search was about to be made, he immured him in a dungeon, a secret place, and sealed it up. And when there would come up strange, mournful sounds from that dungeon, he had it opened and went in and by all kinds of maltreatment sought to silence the voice of the brother crying for help.

But after a while exposure came, the prince was brought up from the pit where he had been immured, and the clear light of day was turned upon the whole transaction in all of its details. The blind brother gave his testimony, reciting how he had been overpowered when asleep; how he had been gagged, so that his voice could not be heard; how imprisoned; how maltreated and subjected to every kind of indignity. On that testimony the younger brother was put to death.

Now that serves as an illustration. There is in every man a dual nature. There is an inner and an outer man. The one entitled to rule is the inner man. The outer man has no qualifications for ruling. He has no judgment. He has no conscience. He is governed by appetite. You may hurt the outer man and the individuality of the inner man is not impaired.

You may destroy both the eyes of the outer man, and the eyes of the inner man can see. You may cut off both hands of the outer man, and the inner man will feel. You may kill the outer man, and the inner man is alive. But any wound to the inner man, the outer man cannot sustain. The inner man can sustain anything put upon the outer one, but it is not so if you reverse it. The spirit of a man sustaineth his infirmities, but a wounded spirit, who can bear?

As an illustration of that Scripture, consider the case of Saul. I have a very special desire in my mind tonight to make a lasting impression upon the minds of some that are here. These two natures were in Saul, king of Israel. He had been instructed that he could not approach God, being a sinner, except through a mediator. He had been assured that if he would follow the divine commandments his kingdom would be established. And yet, in this struggle between the external Saul and the internal Saul he allowed the outer Saul to triumph.

And this text is a confession of what took place. He admits here that God gave him no commandment to offer this sacrifice; that it was not his place. He admits here that he knew he was doing wrong. But he says, "I forced myself." Now, that is very strange language. You see, there is a difference between the "I" and the "myself." There must be two persons or personalities involved in that speech, just as Paul presents it when he says, "That which I would allow not."

Now, in this case Saul allowed the outer man to take violent possession of the inner man; forced him. Here was a suppression of the one who alone had a right to rule. "I forced myself."

And there comes up now the question: What considerations induced Saul to do violence to his spiritual nature? What reasons operated? For evidently he had reasons. Well, he states his reasons. He shows what it was that led him in this instance to force himself to commit a sin. As he states it, three causes conspired to put him in the strait. In the first

place, the Philistines, the enemies of Israel, had massed themselves as a countless multitude—thirty thousand chariots, six
thousand horses, and people as the sands of the seashore.

In the next place, when that formidable host, equipped for
war and conquest, pitched their camp over against him, his
own people were seized with a panic. They fled as birds fly
away from the pursuit and downward swoop of a hawk. They
fled as smaller beasts run away when they hear the roar of
the lion. Every man sought a hiding place. Some went up to
the very mountaintops. Some went into the deepest valleys
and caves, some into the woods, and some fled clear out of the
land across the Jordan. So when Saul looked around, the
people had well-nigh deserted him. So it doubled his em-
barrassment that his crowd was not with him, and the enemy
were present in great numbers, most formidable in their array.
It certainly was an occasion that called for superb courage.

Notice the third element, the representative of God was absent. God's prophet—God's mouth-piece, and therefore you
may say God himself—had directed him to go to this place
where he now was, a place, as you may observe on the map,
of peculiar exposedness, one with few defenses, one which,
without a very strong army to stand by him, seemed to put
him entirely in the hands of his enemies. God had said: "You
go there and wait till I come. Seven days had been appointed.
You wait seven days." Now, the man's courage seemed to
hold out the first day and the second day, though his fears
were rising, and the third, though his fears mounted still
higher, and the fourth, though his heart was up in his mouth;
and the fifth, and the sixth, but the seventh reduced him
to despair.

God was testing him. As if he said: "I will test you to the
very last minutes of the seventh day. I will see what is your
trust in God. I will place you where your foes are in number
like the leaves of the forest trees. I will place you where all
human resources have been dissipated, as dead leaves are
scattered by an autumn blast. I will place you in an exposed

situation, where your only help is God, and then I will see if
you will rely on God."

It seems that Saul was counting the time, not by days only,
but by hours; and before the time fully expired, he suc-
cumbed. But it had almost expired, so that he was within
a very few minutes of deliverance, so that if his patience had
held out just a bit longer, he would live a king, and his children would succeed him upon the throne, and his dynasty
would be perpetuated. Almost victorious. But the shout of
the Philistine hosts terrified him. The continually diminish-
ing numbers of his adherents filled him with fears, and at last,
without a mediator, and in express violation of a divine commandment, he himseslf offered the sacrifice, and sought God
directly face to face.

The inner man protested; the inner man said, "Wait, the
time is not altogether expired. God keeps his appointments."
The inner man stoutly resisted, for when you use the term
"force," then you imply not merely a verbal protest, but an
actual wrestling for supremacy. There was fought a battle.
That inner man and that outer man grappled, and one said,
"Wait on God." And the other said: "The enemy is coming;
I cannot wait." And, as in the story I cited, the younger
brother, the one without any qualifications of ruling, the one
who had no reason and no judgment, bound the elder and
forced him to subordination, and Saul was lost. The spirit
of the man was maltreated. The cowardly body was tri-
umphant. The carnal man reigned and the soul went down
in the conflict.

And, ah! sad commentary upon the situation—no sooner had
the act of violence been perpetrated than the representative
of God stepped upon the scene. "I am here on time. This is
the seventh day; it is not all gone. I am here to deliver you.
And what is that host of Philistines before the Almighty? And
what signifies the fewness of human supporters to God? Have
you forgotten the facts of the history of your people? Have
you not seen one slay a thousand and two put ten thousand

to flight when God was with them? Have you forgotten how
Gideon with his lamps and pitchers discomfited a mighty host
of the enemy? Have you forgotten God's deliverance in
Egypt, in the wilderness, in the establishment of his people
here in this land, in the history of Joshua and the records of
the Judges? Oh, Saul, why could you not have held out just
a little while longer? What is this that thou hast done?"
says Samuel.

"I forced myself. Fear came on me, fear of the enemy,
fear on account of the few that stood with me, fear that you
would not come. I forced myself." And now comes the
dreadful question, the wounded spirit—for the spirit was
wounded in that overthrow—who can bear it?

The sequel is sad indeed. See how that spirit was left alone.
God recalled his Spirit. God refused to communicate with
him. The oracle was dumb when he stood before it, and on
his own unaided resources he had to meet situations with which
he could not cope. And at last that wounded spirit began
to turn in other directions for help; called superstition to its
aid; tried to raise the dead and bring from the silence of the
grave the voice of a buried Samuel.

That wounded spirit said, "Bring me music that hath charms
to soothe the savage breast. Play skillfully on the harp. Let
me hear the sweet melody of poesy. Let me hear the rhythm
and harmony of sweet sounds. Oh, beguile this evil spirit.
Bring something that can make my wounded spirit whole."
"A wounded spirit; who can bear it?"

We trace the history of the man until we see him die on
the field of battle, and with him, his sons; and so perished his
dynasty. His body is gibbeted and exposed. The birds of
carrion come down and fatten upon his flesh. Good men
mourned over him as Samuel had grieved over him before he
died. The old man wept until God called him home, for Saul
had been a kingly man. It was an awful ruin. It was enough
to excite commiseration and melancholy and provoke tears
and grief, to look upon the mighty fallen.

David, Saul's successor, wept. He bemoaned in matchless pathos how that mighty one had fallen. And how piteous to think that, having withstood the temptation one day, two days, three, four, five, six, seven days almost, but the last few moments he allowed his fears to triumph, "and, wrestling with his soul, threw it, and forced it."

Let us look at this subject in some of its general features. That is the history of that case. Whoever is lost in this world is lost somewhat in that way. I do not say that in every case it is fear that causes a man to force himself to sin. Some men are forced that way. Some men lose their self-poise and become panic-stricken, and in the midst of great emergencies, fail to show themselves worthy and succumb to pressure and lose an opportunity of immortality.

But it is not always just that way. Mark you the element of unbelief that made such fear possible. And there you get at the secret of the fall. Why had he not faith in God? Why did his soul accuse God of lying in not keeping his appointment? Why did he think God was trifling when he gave a positive commandment as to how he should be approached? Why did he sit in judgment on God's method of a sinner's coming into his presence? Oh, the infidelity and the presumption that weakened his spirit, so that when fear came, his soul was not able to stand in its wrestling with the outer man.

Unbelief! And I venture to say that, whatever may be the immediate or proximate cause of any man's downfall, the prime cause, the one that made the other possible, is unbelief in God. See a youth fall. See him force himself. Not this time through fear, but because the devil has presented to him pleasure in its most alluring guise: "Here, look at this. This is present; this is real; see this. Why will you not reach out your hand and pluck such luscious fruit within your grasp?"

And the inner man says, "No; God has forbidden me to eat that fruit. God has said that whosoever eateth of the fruit of that tree shall die." "But it is beautiful to the sight and it is sweet to the taste and," says the tempter, "it has power to make one wise that eats it. It will open your eyes and give you knowledge, experimental knowledge of the difference between the good and evil." "Shall I not take God's word that there is a deep and dark chasm between good and evil?" Says Satan: "Pluck the fruit and eat it, and you will know by experience the difference between good and evil." So he yielded to the voice of the devil and fell.

And there comes in unbelief. "Has God said that you will die? You will not surely die. God will not slay you. Believe it not. Doubt it, doubt it. Doubt and pluck and eat." And so unbelief opens the gate through which inordinate desire comes in like a flood and sweeps away every barrier of resistance, and he forces himself. The spirit is wounded, and then who can bear that wounded spirit?

Another time temptation comes with love of money, and so it comes with any other form with which Satan proposes to tempt and wreck a soul, and when it does come, mark you, the wail of that soul can never reproach the Philistines, nor justify itself by saying, "My friends left me, and thereby they slew me." Never. It is always, "I forced myself. I put the dagger to my heart. I put the torch to the beautiful structure of hope and burnt it down and found only despair in its ashes. I doubted."

And therefore the declaration of God is, "Thou hast destroyed thyself." There must be your consent, your yielding, and though ten thousand oceans join, and all the storms that ever rocked their waves had come in one tempest to stir them and roll their mountainous and thunderous tides against your heart, no wave could enter in unless you got scared and opened the floodgate, unless you forced yourself. That is the indictment.

I will refer to only two other points. Are there not at least two ways in which this destruction may come upon me and in which I will be guiltless? Suppose I am but one of thousands, a vast multitude, and but one impulse moves it and that impulse contravenes a commandment of God; am I not guiltless

if such a tide carries me away? May I not innocently refuse
to hear the voice of the inner man which says, "Don't! Don't!
Don't follow a multitude to evil"? Never imagine you can
lose your individuality in a crowd. God Almighty holds you
responsible and his judgment isolates you from the crowd,
segregates you from your companions. Suffer not yourselves
to be deceived by such a device of Satan.

I refer to only one other point. Can I not lose responsibility in corporate capacity? May I not, when comes the issue,
refer responsibility to the corporation which has no soul? God
says, "Come out; be separate. Touch not the unclean thing,"
for if your soul goes down in that wrestling, when the story
is told, when the inscription is written, when your obituary
notice is penned by the unerring angel who, under God's direction, records the facts, it will be just like it was before—"You
forced yourself." And surely, if there are any cases known
to men where a spirit may divest itself of individual responsibility, it is where a multitude is pursuing evil, or it is where,
on account of some complicated association, the conscience is
stifled. Oh, the depths of Satan, the depths of Satan!

And now, having given you the case, I want to tell you
something about what a wounded spirit is. I want you to see
in what somber hues it is painted. When you see it in gospel
colors, you will shudder; you will shiver here in your seat
tonight. It will be like uncapping a pit. It is an awful sight
to look upon a wounded spirit.

Let us see then. That wounded spirit has memory. It
always recollects, not merely the facts in the case, but the
possible facts. When you come to look back upon a sin like
Saul's, you see at last how unnecessary it was. You had
reached the very rim of success without it and there was just
a thin line between you and victory. You had lifted your foot
to place it on the last round of the ladder between you and
the portal of heaven, and from that great height you fell and
fell forever. And oh, that burning reflection, "It might have

been, it might have been!" Forever does that refrain smite you with sadness: "It might have been."

Oh, heaven, heaven! I saw you once, almost touched your portals. I had reached out my hand; I had lifted my foot, and there, when so near the kingdom, the devil, climbing after, made a suggestion to me; and there, wrestling, the outer man threw the spirit on the very verge of redemption and I was lost. "Son," says Abraham to the rich man in hell, "remember, remember."

Then look at this: I know that some people never seem to realize why one is summoned to the bar of judgment after his spirit has been in heaven or hell a long time. Well, let me bring out that thought to you a little. Here is this man, lost, suffering immeasurably, and yet not knowing some things, not realizing some things yet. And the judgment day comes and death and hell give up the dead that are in them, and they are gathered before the bar of God—not so much to be tried as that it is the day of revelation of the past righteous judgment of God—the day when God vindicates himself, the day when God extorts from each lost man a full confession of the justice of the demand; the day when all secret things shall be brought to light. The wounded spirit! How it did devote itself to covering up! Oh, how many efforts it put forth to divert attention from the place where the proof of sin was deposited! Cover up, cover up!

Now, that judgment uncovers, that judgment brings out with exactness every offense committed against God, every one. Every idle word, every thought, every imagination of the heart. There they are, brought out, a long, dreadful record of offenses. And mark you, they were there before, but the light didn't shine on them to make even that lost soul see them, not even in hell. But he sees them now, because that record is held up and the light of God's holy law shines on it and brings out its lack of conformity to that law, measures, surveys it in length and breadth, fathoms its depth.

There it is, now you see it! Not through disordered vision
as on earth, not under the guise with which Satan presented
it. Seen as God's law revealed it. Oh, lost soul, look at
that, and then dare to look at God! Hide! Mountains, come
and fall on me! Bury me out of sight! I can't see the face
of the King, having seen my sins exposed as they are in the
sight of God.

Oh, that wounded spirit! Wounded with such wounds!
These javelins, these darts, these poisons, these swords of sin!
Oh, how they do wound! Pierced through with darts a thou-
sand times. Wounded, and who can bear it?

Yonder on earth where you were covering up and diverting
attention, there still was that Spirit of God who could change
all, but now, never, never. No change now, none, forever.
Can't somebody pray for me? No, not now. Is there no
mercy seat in hell? None, none. What are these things that
rise up yonder? What are they that blacken all the skies
of hope? Clouds of apprehension, fearful looking, forebod-
ing the wrath of God. Wrath, and I have known it. This is
eternal, the wrath of God. Oh, why does my spirit go back
into the past? Oh, that I had no memory! And what is this
that gnaws me? Remorse, undying remorse.

And what is this that keeps echoing in my ear, "I might
have been in heaven"? God called me. God held out to me
pleading hands and bade me come, but I forced myself. My
outer man took possession of my soul and bound it hand and
foot and put out its eyes, and now when I stand before the
judgment bar of God, my conscience, that had been gagged,
my conscience that had been immured in a dark dungeon, my
conscience that had been seared, is called up before that place
where I had bound it and imprisoned it.

God says, "Bring on the witnesses," and here comes the
brother whose eyes had been put out; here comes the one
that should reign, and God says, "Speak and let the court
hear thy voice." And the conscience says, "True and righteous
altogether, Lord God, are thy judgments."

The heart condemns it, echoing the thunders of the divine law—"I destroyed myself." To me it becomes more awful every time I think about it. Any battle where great interests hinge upon its issue is a wonderful thing to study, to see that striving for the mastery, the soul and the carnal man in desperate conflict for supremacy, and at last they totter here and there and one falls. O which? Which is down? Which is on top? Which is overpowered? What a question!

Now the remedy is just this, just what it was to Saul, that God is coming at the appointed time. Do not doubt. God is coming with power of deliverance. Believe him. God is mightier than the Philistines. Never question. God is more than a multitude of men to stand by you as a friend. Never raise the slightest question as to the truth of it. If God be for us, who can be against us? Who? Who from down yonder? Who from here? What force in nature? Lord, thy word, that is law. Lord, thy presence, that is power. Lord, thy promise, that is rescue. Thy blood of redemption, that is salvation. Come to it tonight.

X

THE MARTYRDOM OF JOHN THE BAPTIST

Scripture Lessons: Matthew 14:1-2; Mark 6:14-29; Luke 3:19, 20; 9:7-9.

FROM the concurrent records of Matthew, Mark, and Luke, just read from the revised text in your hearing, I wish to lead you abruptly into a mental picture gallery. Imagine yourselves, therefore, to be in a quiet, ancient hall, bare of all furniture and ornament whatever, whose emptiness and stillness are tenanted by a solitary painting, vast in outline and complex in scenes. The more prominent scene is a palace in lofty Macherus from whose battlements one's view sweeps the far-stretching sands of Arabia, while another looks down on the desolations of the Dead Sea silently shrouding the fate of Sodom and Gomorrah. The far-off background scene embraces dimly the Sea of Galilee and its western fringe of cities.

The first scene reveals the death of John the Baptist. The second reveals the annunciation of that fact to Jesus by the sadhearted disciples of John. All the accessory human forms in the painting are dimly shadowed. But the five principal faces are so clearly outlined by the artist's skill you feel their presence—the faces of Herod, Salome, John the Baptist, Herodias, and Jesus.

Herod's face, overshadowed by an ominous cloud of superstition and apprehension, marks the play of many passions and emotions striving for mastery. Drunkenness, fear, perplexity, shame, pride, and horror all are there.

The face of the dancing girl glows with exercise and gratified vanity. The eyes, void of the light of conscience, gleam like the orbs of a panther cub. She is a playful, voluptuous animal, unconscious of a resident, imprisoned soul.

The face of Herodias is that of a panther dam—old in wickedness and terrible in cruelty. She is fallen beyond all hope of reformation. She no longer debates a moral question. To her ambitious and lust-corroded soul, aflame with the heat of deadly hate, there never come any of the perplexities, superstitions, fears, and remorseful pangs which harass her weaker paramour. She can patiently wait her convenient season. She can seem asleep as she crouches in the path of her victim. But the gleam which shoots from her half-closed eyes is ever vigilant and pitiless. Let Pompeii ask mercy of Vesuvius in eruption—let a baby cradled in a birch canoe plead with Niagara or the maelstrom to forego its suction—let shipwrecked and ice bound mariners in seas implore Winter in his northern home to stay his rigor—but let no man vainly dream that such a woman will fail to fully glut her vengeance when the hour of vengeance comes.

The face of John the Baptist is rigid. The eyes are sightless. The tongue is dumb. The seal of death has shut out vision from the eye and shut off utterance and eloquence from the tongue. The unlighted, vacant, inanimate clay makes no protest against indignities offered.

The face of Jesus, outlined amid shadowy forms, turns toward Macherus from far-off Galilee. There is sympathy for John's bereaved disciples expressed like a benediction in his extended hand of welcome and protection. The glance towards the foe is stern and high. A light shadow forecasting his own doom rests on his brow. But over all and in all is the conscious, pervasive divinity which calmly discerns the yet future but certain rewards and retributions. Let these five faces be the text. Fix the eyes of your soul on them as I briefly recount the necessary historical facts. First make clear to yourselves

THE HERODS OF THE NEW TESTAMENT

The Bible and Josephus mention so many Herods you are liable to have your minds confused. Count it a surname, like Pharaoh or Caesar. Many Pharaohs—many Caesars—many

Herods. Herod the Great, Herod Antipas, Herod Philip, Herod Agrippa, and others. Now to clarify matters somewhat, open your New Testament and follow and mark the several statements. Let us commence with Matthew 2:1: "Now when Jesus was born . . . in the days of Herod the king," and Luke 1:5: "There was in the days of Herod the king of Judaea, a certain priest named Zacharias."

This is Herod the Great, the founder of the family, who rebuilt the temple. It is easy to distinguish him from all others. He was old and near his death when Jesus was born. He is the one who murdered the little children in Bethlehem, hoping thereby to destroy the infant Jesus. You see an account of his death in the same chapter (Matthew 2:19) while Jesus is yet an infant in Egypt. Of course, therefore, he is not the Herod of our theme today, for Jesus and John are now grown men, one ending, the other in the midst of his public ministry.

The first Herod was really a king and a great man. None of the others was really great. This first Herod married five times. All these wives, Doris, Mariamne (granddaughter of Hyrcanus, last of the Maccabees), Mariamne (daughter of Simon), Malthace (a Samaritan woman), and Cleopatra bore him children. He himself put to death his sons by the first two wives, and disinherited the son (Herod Philip) by his third wife.

Neither Mark nor John has anything to say about Herod the Great. Now fix this fact in your mind: When the first Herod died his dominions were partitioned by will among his sons by the last two wives.

Archelaus, a son by the fourth wife, had Judea with Jerusalem for his capital. When Archelaus died, which was before Jesus was grown, the Romans appointed governors over Judea, called procurators, as Pontius Pilate (Matthew 27:2), Felix (Acts 23:24), Porcius Festus (Acts 24:27).

Herod Antipas, another son by the fourth wife, had Galilee and Perea. This is the Herod of our theme today.

See how clearly Luke distinguishes between the father and son. One is "Herod the king of Judaea"; the other, "Herod the tetrarch of Galilee" (Compare Luke 1:5 with 3:1). You may distinguish this Herod from all others as the murderer of John the Baptist and as the one who made friends with Pilate for recognizing his jurisdiction over Jesus as a Galilean (Luke 23:7-12). It is this Herod who divorced his own wife to marry Herodias, the wife of his disinherited elder brother, Herod Philip I.

Herod Philip I, son of the fifth wife, had Iturea and Trachonitis (See Luke 3:1). This is the Herod who built Caesarea Philippi (mentioned in Matthew 16:13). In the New Testament he is called Philip. But you must be careful not to confound him with his older brother, also named Philip, who was the husband of Herodias (See Luke 3:19-20). This Herod Philip married, not Herodias, but Salome, the girl who danced off the head of John the Baptist, though Salome is herself sometimes called Herodias, her mother's name.

Herod Agrippa I was the grandson of Herod the Great, nephew of the Herod who killed John the Baptist, brother of Herodias and hence, by marriage, brother-in-law of his uncle. Through his influence at Rome, the Herod who killed John the Baptist was deposed and banished. Also through his popularity at Rome, he finally obtained possession of all his grandfather's dominions. He is the Herod of Acts 12:1 who killed James the apostle and imprisoned Peter, and whose blasphemy was punished by the awful death mentioned in Acts 12:23.

Herod Agrippa II, son of Herod Agrippa I and great grandson of Herod the Great, is the one before whom Paul makes his great defense, commencing, "I think myself happy, king Agrippa," etc. (Acts 26:2). His sisters were Drusilla, married to Felix (Acts 24:24) and Bernice (Acts 25:23). How then may you easily distinguish between the Herods of the New Testament?

Herod the Great, who murdered the children in Bethlehem, seeking to destroy Jesus (Matthew 2:16).

Herod Philip I, the disinherited son of Herod the Great by wife three, first husband of his niece Herodias (Luke 3:19).

Herod Antipas, tetrarch of Galilee and Perea, son of Herod the Great by wife four, who took his brother Philip's wife, Herodias, who killed John the Baptist, who mocked Jesus and made friends with Pilate (Luke 23:6-12).

Herod Philip II, tetrarch of Iturea (Luke 3:1), son of Herod the Great by the fifth wife, who married his niece, Salome, the dancing girl.

Herod Agrippa I, king of Judea, grandson of Herod the Great, his father being son of Herod the Great by second wife. He is the Herod of Acts 12:1-23, who killed the apostle James, imprisoned Peter and was himself struck by an angel and eaten of worms.

Herod Agrippa II, son of the foregoing, before whom Paul pleaded (Acts 26).

With this glance at the Herod family, let us resume our subject. In one verse of Luke's Gospel we have a summary of the political situation, "Now in the fifteenth year of the reign of Tiberius Caesar, Pontius Pilate being governor of Judaea, and Herod being tetrarch of Galilee, and his brother Philip tetrarch of the region of Iturea and Trachonitis, and Lysanias, tetrarch of Abilene" (Luke 3:1).

Note on a map that the part assigned to Herod was Galilee and Perea. Perea was east of the river Jordan, and reached down to the upper part of the Dead Sea, and connected with Arabia.

Now as Jesus lived most of his time in Galilee, he lived in the district that was under Herod's jurisdiction, and most of his mighty work was done close by Herod's home, the city of Tiberius, on the Sea of Galilee, but when Herod went over into Perea, the other section of country under his jurisdiction, his capital was Macherus, about nine miles north of the upper part of the Dead Sea, and just on the border of Arabia.

Here was an immensely high hill, the top of it a plain, and from that plain there went up another part very high, and on top of that highest part was a citadel, and under that citadel, dungeons, deep dungeons in the rock.   They are there now, and in that dungeon on the top of that high hill in the capital of Perea, there John the Baptist died.

Now, you will understand that Herod never could have put to death John the Baptist if he had remained in Judea, for Judea was not under Herod's jurisdiction, but we learn that John went over into Perea, and he was baptizing in Perea. That brought him into Herod's jurisdiction, and close to Herod, and hence it would be legal for Herod to arrest him.

The question now comes up: What occasioned a meeting between Herod and John?   Herod would never go to hear John preach, that is, in public places, where the people heard him; of course not.   How, then, did John and Herod ever get together?   This way, as I think: Herod had a use for John and the use was this: Herod had married a daughter of a king of Arabia, a country lying right next to Perea.   He went to the city of Rome on some business, and while there, stopped with his disinherited elder brother, Herod Philip I, and fell in love with his brother's wife, Herodias.   Herodias, seeing that her husband had been disinherited, having neither property nor a princely title, and being very ambitious, divorced her husband on condition that Herod would divorce his wife, so these two could marry.   And so there, while a guest of his brother, partaking of his hospitality, this infamous agreement was reached between this man and this woman, and they married.

When he came back to Judea with this wife, having sent his first wife to her father, there arose two troubles.   First, Aretas, the king of Arabia, justly very much incensed at the indignity put upon his daughter, began to raise an army for attacking Herod and soon afterward did attack him, and but for the intervention of the Romans, Herod's government would have been swept from the face of the earth. That trouble was pending and caused Herod much anxiety.

The other trouble was that the conscience of the Jewish nation revolted at this infamous marriage. He had in two notorious particulars violated their law. In the first place, Herodias was Herod's niece, and therefore any marriage to her, under any circumstances, would have been violative of the Mosaic law, but mainly she was the wife of his brother, and that brother was living. The only instance in the Bible where a woman divorces her husband is this case. That could be done in Rome, but it could not be done in Judea. Among the Jews, the husband could divorce, but not the wife. Doubtless Mark 10:12 was meant for the Gentiles.

Now the Jewish conscience rose up in rebellion against such an iniquity. Here was a governor of Galilee and Perea, the head man of the nation, living in open violation of a fundamental law, threatening the Jews with unnecessary war. Their indignation threatened to break out in open revolt. Hence Herod, seeing the approach of a formidable external enemy, was much embarrassed by feeling insecure of support from his own people, whose conscience had been shocked by this marriage. He must see to it that both evils did not come at once. Herod, whom Jesus calls the fox, cunning like, fell upon an expedient to get himself out of this trouble.

Here had come over to his country John the Baptist, a great man, a wonderful prophet, and all the people united in one thing, that John was the holiest man of his day. He was great. His word was more potent in governing the ideas of the people than a proclamation of the king. I mean the masses of the people, and it was upon the masses that Herod had to rely in this extremity. So he sends for John to get John to endorse this marriage. He thought, "Now, if I get John here in my palace, in the presence of Herodias, and he looks in the face of this grandly beautiful woman, the queen, that sits by my side, he, a rough country man, who has never been in the presence of a king, where people wear soft cloth-

ing; he, accustomed to dress in rough camel's hair garments
—if I get him here in the midst of the pomp and splendor of
the court, and he can see what power I have to promote him,
and I say, 'John, spread the mantle of your approbation over
this marriage of mine,' the masses will be influenced by John
and what he says, and I can at least appease the home opposition, and be better prepared to meet Aretas on the battle-
field."

John comes and the case is put before him. What did he
say? He rises like Elijah. He stands up in all the sublimity
of the attitude of that ancient prophet of God who confronted
the priests of Baal, who rebuked Ahab and Jezebel, and shak-
ing his finger in the face of Herod, said: "It is not lawful
for you to have your brother's wife." As if he had said: "I
am poor; I have nothing in this world, but you, with all of
your wealth and power, cannot bribe me or my conscience to
say that you are living righteously in the sight of God."

Nor did he stop at that. Luke says he went on; he made it
the occasion of preaching a sermon on the sins of Herod.
Luke says he told Herod of all the evil things he had been
doing. You will find that in Luke 3:19-20. He lifted the
veil off Herod's tortuous life. He caused each dark sin to rise
up before him, and there, faithful to his God and to the
truth, with a courage that has never been surpassed, knowing
what would be the penalty, standing alone, surrounded by the
court of the tyrant and his guards, he rebuked sin in high
places, knowing that if the leaders sinned, demoralization
would spread throughout all the ramifications of society.

He was not of the number that select some weakling without
friends and arraign him. He spoke to the chief sinners, the
Pharisees that were at the head of ecclesiastical affairs, to
Herod, the ruler of this Jewish people, as if he had said: "If
you, the ruler of this people, violate a plain law of God and
live a life of shame and infamy, what is to become of the
country? Will not all the weak pattern after the ruler? Is
it not the custom for those who wish to stand well with author-

ity to imitate the manners and customs of the rich and great
and those who are in position? For the sake, then, of truth,
for the sake of the people, for the sake of God's high and holy
law, I impeach you as a tyrant, as an adulterer and as a cunning, scheming, fraudulent impostor, and arraign you before
the bar of God, where you shall stand and be judged."

Well, you can imagine the effect of such testimony. It
shocked Herod off his base. He was terribly offended, but
nevertheless he was wonderfully struck with the character of
such a man, and if left to himself, perhaps would have said,
"John, you are a great man. I know that what you say is
true, but I cannot follow it." But sitting by the side of Herod
was one whose heart had also been laid bare by this denun-
ciation of John—Herodias. And when John denounced her,
she set her heart against him, and whenever a woman is bad,
she is always worse than a man. Generally a woman is far
better than a man, but when she begins to go down in iniquity,
she fixes no limit. She goes always and forever down; and
in her heart she determined that that witness against her sin
should die.

Here was the sin and there was the man exposing it; here
was the iniquity and there was the witness to the iniquity.
Here was the transgressor and there was the vindicator of the
violated law, and she said he must die. She demanded of
Herod that he should die. Herod said, "You cannot put him
to death; he told the truth; you know it and I know it, that
we are living in sin, and I will keep you from killing him."

Will he? When did ever a wicked man keep a wicked woman
from doing what she intended? "How will I keep you from
killing him? Up yonder is a citadel, and no one is ever
allowed to enter it; that citadel is under the control of my
creatures; down under its foundations are deep dungeons that
never see light. I will put John there, and how will you get
him?" The woman smiled and waited. She said nothing at
the time, but she knew Herod. "I can't get Herod to do this

while sober; I cannot induce him in his normal state, in his right mind, to kill John, but I will watch and wait."

When a man is wicked, in some hour of weakness you can find a way to work your purpose with him, if he throws off the restraints of the divine law. If he does not allow God to prescribe the rule of moral actions, none of his protests against greater wickedness will avail him anything. He may say, "I know I am bad, but I won't go that far. I am perplexed when I hear John preach," and he would slip off to that dungeon and say, "Talk to me again, John."

The original Greek text certainly intimates that there were many interviews between John and Herod. The tense expresses continued conversations. He would slip off from his wife, drawn by a strange kind of fascination, to hear a man talk that feared not the power of kings, that, though alone and unsupported, would speak out for the truth. He was an original speaker and thinker. There was a sublimity about his character that this weak, vacillating man found to be very attractive, and so he would hear John, and there in that dungeon, the voice of God would speak to Herod, through John: "Herod, you are living in sin; you are living in open and shameful violation of God's laws. Is it true?" "Yes." "Ought you to do it?" "No." "Will you quit this?" Now listen: "And he was much perplexed." The perplexity that comes to a weak man, a wicked man, a man who has discrimination enough to know right from wrong, a man whose conscience and judgment will approve the right, and yet who is not prepared to give up sin. There comes his perplexity.

And I want to make this one observation, that to a man who knows and approves the right but will not do it, to that man all life is a perplexity; all life and death and eternity are problems. He will find himself continually agitated in mind, duty pointing in one direction, conscience approving of doing duty, and inclination turning him in another direction—a divided mind.

The connection tells of another perplexity that came to him later. I shall refer to that directly. Now mark, here was a man who had gone certain lengths in sin, but was not prepared to go other lengths; here was a woman who, having gone so far, was more logical. "Having descended this distance, why not descend all distances? Why set up any barriers? Why set up any limit? This man denounced us. This man must die."

The record says that when a convenient day came—convenient to whom? Not to Herod, not to John, but to that woman. What was the convenient day? It was an occasion that the devil often uses for such purposes—a birthday celebration. Do you know that more men lose their souls on occasions of celebration, on great festive occasions, than on all the funeral occasions in the world? At that time a man is weak. At that time his heart is given up wholly to joy and pleasure.

A boy says about Christmas: "Now, Christmas comes but once a year; ordinarily I would not think of such a thing." But how adroitly the devil waits for the convenient time— "here, let's have an egg-nog today. I know you never drink, but this is Christmas day (or a birthday) and this is a festive occasion." One hour of weakness may cause the downfall of one who has stood the test of a thousand ordinary temptations. It would be an interesting thing, if I had the time, to relate the many instances that occur to me, mentioned in history, of souls lost on their birthdays or other festivals.

Well, this day comes, and Herod has all of the chief men of Galilee and Perea about him, and you can see from reading this context just how drunk he was. The tense indicates that he kept swearing that he would give this girl anything she asked him. Now, a sober man who has been pleased and who wishes to make a gift will state it in quiet language and be done with it, but if a man is excited by a stimulant, he will keep on saying, "I will give you whatever you want," and keep on saying, "I'll give you anything you ask me, to the half of my kingdom." You can see from the record that he is drunk.

Well, this waiting woman knew this. She reasoned with herself: "When Herod becomes merry with liquor, and mellow, I'll strike for John the Baptist." The first sacrifice she made—listen at this emphasis—"the daughter of Herodias herself came and danced." Why does the Scripture say that? Why does it say the daughter of Herodias "herself" came in and danced? Because no reputable woman danced, either in Judea or in Rome. To be a dancing woman announced that you were either a slave, bought with some man's money, or that you were fallen, and when the men were at their banquets they made their women slaves come in and dance. It was an act of utter and inexcusable indecency for this woman to make her daughter go in and dance before that drunken company. "No, I have an object to accomplish. That man rebuked my sin. He must die."

Do you remember a similar instance with which she was doubtless quite familiar? She had lived at Rome. She was living at Rome when she first met Herod, and not a very great while before this, Fulvia, the wife of Antony, had heard that Cicero, in the senate, rebuked and excoriated Antony; had heard that Cicero pleaded for Roman freedom against Octavius and Antony, and Fulvia said, "Cicero shall die." And when men were willing to forgive Cicero, she said, "I will never rest until I have his head. Give me nothing but Cicero's head." And when the head of the great Roman orator was brought to her in a dish, she pryed the mouth open and drew out the tongue that had denounced her husband, and drove her hairpin through it repeatedly and spat in the cold face: "You speak again against my husband!"

That is where Herodias got her idea, and Jerome, one of the early fathers of the church, declares upon authority that he had, which we have not, that, when the head of John the Baptist was brought as the most palatable dish that could be presented from Herod's table to this woman, she pryed open his mouth and drew out that dumb tongue which had denounced her crime, and, in imitation of Fulvia, drove her hairpin repeatedly through it. "And the daughter of Herodias herself came in and danced." "In order to have my vengeance, I will sacrifice my daughter's reputation. I will make her take a place of indecency. I will make her take a position that will announce to the world that she is either a slave or a fallen woman."

So far the daughter had not been taken into the mother's confidence. I know that in the English version of one Gospel it says she that had before been instructed of her mother, but it is not so in the text, and two of the Gospel histories state distinctly that when Herod kept repeating, "I swear I will give you anything, to the half of my kingdom, if you ask it," (he had no kingdom), she ran in and submitted the case to her mother: "Mother, what shall I ask him?" That was a filial thing to do. Who would forbid a daughter on any occasion going to her mother and saying, "Mother, what shall I ask?"

Now notice: "Go back in a hurry and tell him to give you immediately," that is what Mark says, "instantly," "the head of John the Baptist in one of the dishes there on the table (one of those huge dishes). They are at a feast. I am not permitted to go and sit at that feast, and I want something sent to me, a delicacy, and what I ask for is the head of my enemy. Go and tell him to send me instantly the head of John the Baptist."

Why instantly? "When Herod becomes sober, he will not kill John. If I strike at all, it must be now. This is the convenient time. It may never come again. It is here now. He is committed by a promise. He has confirmed that promise by an oath. This oath was public. It was made in the presence of the members of his court, and he is a weak man, and no weak man wishes to be thought weak. He wishes to seem consistent, and I know it, and if he will say anything and swear to it, and swear to it publicly, he is too weak to refuse to keep his promise, and I must strike him while he is drunk." That is the reason of the haste.

Now look, I want you to see it—that great company of men —you see the long table, you see the viands on the table, you see the wines and strong drinks, you see the drunken men there, and standing just as she had danced is the girl there, in the costume for such a dance, silent—waiting for what? Herod turns around to the guard: "Go at once and bring me the head of John the Baptist," and the girl and the company stand silent. That interval! Oh! Let it be impressed upon your minds—waiting, and directly the guard comes in, and there on the bloody dish is the head of the man of whom Jesus said none greater than he had ever been born of woman. A girl holding such a dish! And she carried it to her mother!

There she, the imitator of Fulvia, spits in the cold face of God's dead prophet. See her try to put an indignity upon that tongue that, while the soul warmed the body, no king's chains could bind. "Thou didst rebuke my sins—I have thy head." And yet, in putting to death that witness, she but filled the whole earth with the sound of her crime. By that barbarous execution, her adultery, which was known in limited circles only, was advertised to the ends of the earth, and age after age, and age after age, until eternity shall come. Wherever the Book goes, into ten thousand languages translated, and wherever men preach to nations then or yet unborn, they hold up before the world the sins of this woman who thought by the death of John to silence the testimony against her crimes.

Now notice again: Jesus had come over into Perea about this time. That is what the preceding context intimates. He is now not very far from Macherus. He had but recently sent out his apostles. They went abroad working miracles, and his fame fills the land, and Herod hears it. Now let us suppose it is night. Herod is trying to sleep—he who has murdered sleep—and while he tries to sleep, he hears a soft falling footstep, and there glides into his room an apparition, which parts the curtains of his bed, and before him is the dancing girl with the head of John the Baptist in a dish.

So his superstitious fear cries out: "This new man that has come into Perea, into the same places from which I called John, must be John the Baptist risen from the dead. I did not silence him. I thought to silence him. I thought to put the seal of death on his dumb lips, but my conscience arouses me at night and tells me that this is John the Baptist, who was put to death." Now what does he do? Well, you have only to read a little further on to see. He did one of the slyest things. He did a thing that made Jesus call him a fox. His conscience was hurting him.

Now, we see where that second perplexity comes in: "And when Herod heard of the works of Jesus, he was much perplexed, and he said, 'This is John the Baptist risen from the dead.'" Perplexed when he heard John and would not do right; perplexed again when the works of Jesus make him think that it is John risen from the dead. That perplexity will never leave him. Like a tangled web will be his mind as long as he lives, perplexed living and perplexed dying, until the judgment ends all of his earthly perplexity.

Well, what did he do? "Since putting a man to death does not silence him and end his testimony, I have tried that, and now here he has risen from the dead—now what?" He called to his side some Pharisees (in the thirteenth chapter of Luke, you will find it) and said: "You go yonder where Jesus is preaching; don't let him know it came from me, but do you go and say to him, 'Get up and get out of this country, for Herod would fain kill you,'" trying to scare Jesus out of the country, resorting to a trick to scare him! And so when the Pharisees came where Jesus was preaching, prompted by this guilty conscience of Herod that made him think that Jesus was John the Baptist risen from the dead, they said to Jesus, "Get up and get out of this country, for Herod would fain slay thee." Jesus turned and said: "You go and tell that fox that I will be here today, tomorrow, and next day." As if he said: "I see through the strategem. I know who sent you. You go tell that fox that I will remain here till my time comes to depart."

And now we can see how rapidly approaches the doom of Herod. Soon after, he was defeated in battle by Aretas. Some years afterward his nephew, Herod Agrippa I (the Herod of Acts 12:1 who murdered James and imprisoned Peter) begins to supplant him. His wife urges him to go to Rome to obtain from the emperor the kingly title over all the country. But the nephew was also a fox, and he sent word to Rome, too, such a catalogue of Herod's crimes, that Herod was not only not made king, but was deposed from his tetrarchy and banished into Spain.

At this juncture occurs the only favorable thing recorded in history about this woman. The Emperor of Rome offered her a large annuity and the title of princess, but she declined both and went into exile with Herod and died with him.

Now look again at the painting. Contrast the faces. There is Herod. Count the steps of his downfall. Through lust and ambition he marries his brother's wife. Rebuked for that sin, he imprisoned the witness against the sin. Having imprisoned the witness, he becomes drunk on a public occasion, swears repeatedly that he will do a certain thing. Bound by that oath, as he thought, he yielded to its requirements and committed murder. Afterward he sees in every good man that passes through the country John the Baptist risen from the dead. War comes and smites him. His people rise up and denounce him. His emperor deposes and banishes him, and far away in a foreign land, in a place almost unknown, in obscurity, he ends his days. He and his wife end their days on earth, to meet God and John the Baptist in the hereafter, at the judgment.

Look at John. See the colossal man. Five distinct prophecies point to him. Isaiah, seven hundred years before, had told about him as a voice in the wilderness: "Prepare ye the way of the Lord and make straight his paths." Malachi, four hundred years before, had seen him as a messenger of the Lord, coming in the spirit and power of Elijah. The angel prophesied about him when he stood in the Temple by the side of his father and announced his birth. The father prophesied about him on the eighth day after his birth, as the spirit of inspiration rested upon him, and John prophesied about himself. His own prophecy of himself had in it just three words—"I must decrease." "He must increase." "I must decrease."

And there in that castle a great man ended his life. He prepared for it thirty years. He prepared thirty years to do six months' work. Though his public life lasted over two years' time, it culminated when he baptized Jesus Christ. Thirty years' preparation for six months' work! And yet in that six months he was so prepared that he shook the world with his work.

What a lesson to those who run hastily, having nothing to tell, not understanding about what they speak, not having studied under a subject and over it and around it and through it—unprepared.

John prepared by thirty years of self-denial and temperance. He took no wines, no strong drink, temperate in his food, and by meditation and prayer and consecration and communion with God, he filled himself full of his great mission, and when he did speak, he spoke where there was no man in the wilderness and his voice that broke the solitude of that wilderness was so loud and so persuasive and so attractive that it drew to that infrequented and solitary place the population of the country and of the cities, and they came, thousands, massing together there where no synagogue could hold them. No building had walls enough to surround the crowds that came.

This greatest of men—this man that reformed his generation and was the forerunner of the Son of God—fulfilled his course. What if he did die? What if he did die alone? What if he did die in that prison? What if indignities were heaped upon that dead body? He had done his work. He had fulfilled his course. He had made his impress, and this you can say about him: No wealth could bribe him, no power could purchase that unpurchasable soul.

John was a man who had a mission; a man who knew why he lived; a man who left not the chapters of his life to accident; not a reed blown that way by a wind and back again by a contrary wind; not bending as the wind would blow, but a man independent of effeminate life, gluttonous eating, luxurious living; that cared nothing for the circumstances of dress and food and society, but stood upon the incorruptibility of his integrity, upon the greatness of his mission, and who fulfilled that mission. How small is Herod by the side of John!

These are some of the lessons of this Scripture. I pray God that they may reach some hearts here today. I want to make this one application. This is a new year. A long time ago—I do not think I was more than eleven years of age—a man from New England, a teacher of mine, and one of the best teachers I ever knew, on one New Year's day said to me, "Now today, my boy, I want you to fix your mind on definite things. Do not be a dry leaf that this wind will pick up and carry that way, and yonder wind pick up and carry another way—be somebody; have a purpose; preserve your own individuality; do your own thinking; regard the teachings of the Bible, for," said he, "if you are ever whipped in this life, it will be because you are whipped inside. There is the place men are whipped." I never shall forget his language.

Now you look at this man that was whipped inside—this Herod. Why, of course, Aretas, could whip him, and his nephew could whip him, and a dead man could whip him, and a girl could whip him. He was whipped inside. He was purchasable. There was no granite in his character. There was no moral fiber in his being—swayed hither and thither, as influences were brought to bear on him. I do pray to God that if there is in you an inclination to weakness, an inclination to let other people push you where they want you to go, and thrust you into situations that you do not approve of, you will today, for manhood's sake, try to settle one question, come to one resolution: "I will not only be myself, but I never will, God helping me, demoralize myself." I know that that is one thought that comes to me in the darkest situations of my life, and I have been in many a trying place, but I never yet have been in depths so deep nor in situations so unfavorable, but in the darkest hour of it, when I am alone I say to myself: "As far as men are concerned, I will be the master of my own fate. I never will take counsel of my fears. I will not be demoralized."

And now that is what I want you to do. Seek to have character. You cannot sin as Herod sinned and remain strong. You cannot undermine the foundation and leave the house in safety. You cannot honeycomb veracity and remain a brave and true man. Be not a liar, an adulterer, a deceiver, a fraud, or a man that will sell his soul for sixpence in a trade. Touch not, taste not, handle not anything of the unclean things, and resolve this year to live true; live true to God and your conscience, even if it puts you in hard and trying circumstances. Oh, be true to the truth, and to the right, and to God! Then, should you die young, like John the Baptist, you will, like John, fulfil your course.

XI

CHRIST'S GOSPEL TRIUMPHS OVER
ALL ADVERSARIES

TEXT: *But I will tarry at Ephesus until Pentecost; for a great door and effectual is opened unto me, and there are many adversaries.*—1 CORINTHIANS 16:8.
(Scriptures read: Acts 18:18-21; 19:1-41; 17:38; 1 Corinthians 15:32; 2 Corinthians 1:8-10.)

I AM not able physically to preach the sermon that is in my mind on this text, having been quite ill since last Thursday, but as well as I may under the circumstances, I want to call your attention to the salient points of the text.

The Bible history of the case may be gathered from the Scriptures read. Luke tells us (Acts 18:18-21) of Paul's first visit to Ephesus, accompanied by Aquila and Priscilla, his short stay, but active ministrations in the synagogue, the pressing invitation to return, given by the Jews. While Paul is away, Apollos comes from Alexandria, knowing only the baptism of John, and labors in the synagogue, but after being "instructed in the way of the Lord more accurately" by Aquila and Priscilla, departs for Corinth. After long absence Paul returns, and for more than two years labors there as he himself describes in a subsequent address at Miletus to the elders of the church (Acts 20:17-38), and in such perils as he depicts in his great argument on the resurrection (1 Corinthians 15:32) and in his second letter to the church at Corinth (2 Corinthians 1:8-10). All these Scriptures should be carefully compared and studied. Besides this inspired record, profane history and ecclesiastical tradition have much to say about this wonderful place, Paul's more wonderful work and its widespread and long-continued effects.

First, I want to get before you clearly some idea of the scene of this lesson. Asia Minor, bordering on the Mediterranean Sea, was settled largely by colonists from Greece, and Ephesus in particular was settled by a colony of the Athenians. It was at the mouth of a little river that lay between two larger streams, and was on the great thoroughfare of travel between the East and the West, that is, from Rome to Antioch. It was also on the line of sea travel. All vessels navigating the Mediterranean Sea were accustomed to stop at that port, so that it was upon a thoroughfare both by land and sea. It was a very large city and immensely wealthy. This city, so far as religion was concerned, had a garrison of such number and strength that it would seem to be absolutely impregnable by Christian attack. This is referred to under so much of the text as says, "there are many adversaries." I will call your attention to these adversaries in the order in which they are mentioned in the history.

First, there was the adversary of an imperfect knowledge of the gospel of Jesus Christ, as is evidenced in the case of the disciples of John. They had been baptized doubtless by someone who pretended to perpetuate the baptism of John, but John had no successor; he had been dead twenty or twenty-five years; no man was authorized to keep up his mission, and therefore the baptism which they had received was without authority from God. They were wholly ignorant of the fact that the Lord Jesus had come and that he had died and was buried and had ascended into heaven and had sent the Holy Spirit down from heaven. And Paul found these men, and by the instruction of the gospel, he removed the difficulties out of their way. They believed on Jesus as the Messiah, were baptized, and then by the laying on of his hands received the baptism of the Holy Ghost, the miraculous power of speaking with tongues and working miracles.

The second adversary that opposed his progress in this city was a Jewish one. There was a vast number of Jews here, very much attached to the ritual of their fathers. They were the Pharisees, similar to those who held the ecclesiastical as well as much of the civil power in Jerusalem, and it was almost impossible to get a hearing from them outside of their regular lines of thought. You see that when he devoted three months' labor in their synagogue, endeavoring to show them from their own Bible that the Messiah that they looked for had come, that he was Jesus, and that every proof of the Messiah met in him and could meet in no one else, a number of them were converted, but the others, as they did in every other place where he preached, very bitterly opposed his work.

The two lines of thought were irreconcilable—what they thought and preached and what he thought and preached—and whenever that is the case, there is no remedy but a separation. Hence the apostle drew the line of cleavage. He separated the disciples. He said, "You cannot worship here with these people. We will have to go away to ourselves and leave them to themselves." So he found a place where a certain teacher of philosophy, a man by the name of Tyrannus, had a school, and that schoolhouse was opened up to him as a place of preaching. There for two years he preached to the Gentiles, casting out demons.

Here were evil spirits, who had been with Satan, cast out of heaven, and who had obtained possession of the souls of men and dominated their spirits, just like they do now, very largely in Spiritualism, Mormonism, and Mohammedanism. These demons had possession of the souls of men, and they were among the adversaries that Paul had to combat. Not only was this true, but he had to bear a conflict with false exorcists of evil spirits. There were Jews who claimed to have the power to cast out these demons. They agreed with him that demons did take possession of men's minds and did control them, but they claimed that they had the power to exorcise the demons, and they ran an opposition method of exorcism against that exercised by the apostle Paul in the name of the Lord Jesus Christ. When they saw that their method was not as potent as his, they determined that they would continue their work by using the name that he used, the name of Jesus, attaching a magical influence to it, thinking that, if they would simply pronounce it over one who was possessed of a spirit, he would depart.

The idea of a name having this magical power is inwrought in all the Oriental stories. How often you find it in the *Arabian Nights*. How often you find it in Oriental history and legend, such an instance as this, where a magical name is carved on a sword, and whoever carries that sword will conquer. Now, they had such a thought as that, and hence they came to one possessed of evil spirits and tried its magical influence: "We adjure you by the name of Jesus, whom Paul preacheth." But the evil spirit knew Jesus and knew Paul, and did not know them; so he prompted the man to leap on them and seek to destroy them, and so remarkable was this demonstration that it led to the conversion of a great many people, and that adversary was overthrown. So devils are made to testify for Christ.

Another adversary was magic, as connected with idolatrous worship. If I had the time, I could give you a great deal of history and legend on what were called the Ephesian letters. They were used for magical purposes. Two or three letters would be written upon a garment that would be worn next to the skin as an amulet or charm, and were said to be able to protect against any disease or any enemy. You remember that when Croesus was dying, on his funeral pyre he called over the magical Ephesian letters. You remember in another ancient story it is said that a wrestler overcame every adversary until he dropped in the struggle the magical Ephesian letters which had given him his power. Ancient history and legend are full of this.

Now, the apostle Paul preached a gospel that was designed to uproot the very foundation idea of reliance upon magic of any kind. That adversary stood before him and he overwhelmed it by the truth of Jesus Christ. Magic, however, was supported by a literature which expounded it and showed how it was to be made efficacious—marvelous and costly books. And you will find that whenever any sin becomes really formidable, it fastens itself in a literature which is committed to its maintenance, and that before you can ever uproot it you must overturn the literature which sustains it.

The gospel of Jesus Christ came against this magic and its literature; the Book of God against these books. It was a question of power as to which should triumph. Here was a literature that had obtained a power over the minds of men through hundreds of years. It had ruled the souls of kings as well as of slaves. Paul came with the simple gospel of Jesus, and the books fell before the Book of God. They became useless in men's hands. They were shown to be the exponents of error, and those who owned them brought them and piled them up in a heap, and, as the Greek expresses it, kept bringing them and kept piling them and kept burning them, so that the smoke and the sparks and the flames from that conquered literature went up to heaven, and told to the stars that looked down, the mighty power of the gospel of Jesus over the evil literature that there is in this world. It went up as a protest against that evil. It went up as a prophecy which forecast the ultimate destruction of all evil literature.

Every newspaper which advocates a false idea, every book which defends an evil philosophy, every book which is devoted to the inculcation of the doctrines of idolatry and of error of every kind, shall meet the fate of the magician books at Ephesus. If they burn not now, they will burn when God wraps the world in fire, and, with their defenders, shall utterly perish, and this venerable Book shall be lifted above them and be placed on the white throne of the judgment, and shall be the arbiter of their fate,

We notice that the next adversary he had to confront was idolatry; and, brethren, such an idolatry! We cannot realize it now. The ancients had seven great wonders, called the seven wonders of the world. This was one of them—this Temple of Diana at Ephesus. It was four hundred and twenty-five feet long and two hundred and twenty feet wide. It had no roof, but it was a succession of colonnades, pillars standing sixty feet high—marble pillars. There were one hundred and twenty-seven of these marble pillars. A king exhausted his treasury to give each one of them. Some of them were marvelously ornamented, with chapiters at their top, and there was a winding stairway that went up which was one vine that had been cut down in an island of the Mediterranean Sea, and already had the natural curve of a stairway. This was the most magnificent building at that time standing in the heathen world. It was so magnificent that Alexander the Great offered all the spoils of his Eastern conquests if he might carve his name alone on that temple; his offer was declined.

The idolatry of Ephesus is not wholly dead. What was it? It was the worship of a woman. Not that Diana of the Athenian Greeks, the chaste huntress, but a horrid Oriental image, a monstrosity, said to have fallen down from heaven, whose servitors were celibate priests and nuns, with a high priest over them. There substantially was every form that you may witness today in Mexico, in the South American republics, in Spain, in Italy, a woman exalted as God, with priests and nuns, vowed to celibacy, serving at her altars and distributing her images for worship. That was the idolatry that had possession of the Ephesian mind.

This idolatry was linked to commerce. That temple was the treasure house of Asia. All of the surplus gold and silver and jewels of neighboring nations were stored there. It was the great international bank, the place of deposit, and that horrid monster stood over that treasure and guarded it—the treasure of kings and of provinces—and linked itself to every coin that went into circulation, and linked itself to every trade by which men subsisted.

Not only this, but it was an idolatry that attached itself to all the theaters and games and amusements and entertainments of the people. From the height of that temple you looked down on that grand theater where their dramas were performed, and where probably Paul himself was mangled by wild beasts, as a martyr to their hate. You looked out on where their May festivals were held—for they were held in the month of May. The world met there on the first of May to hold their festivals and attend the theater and attend these races and take part in them, and this idolatry was thus attached and linked onto the public games, the public amusements, the public entertainments, as well as the commerce of the world. Not only so, but it had created a ring of craftsmen, whose subsistence depended upon its maintenance—men who made their fortunes by making the models of that image, the miniature silver shrines—little goddesses that you could tie about your neck, that you could carry home and hang up in your room,—so that when you got up in the morning you could bow down before that shrine and pray to that household image. By the manufacture of these images a vast number of silversmiths derived an immense fortune. They had what you know all about in this country, a craftsmen's ring, a trade union, an organization that continually looked to the best interests of that particular union. Idolatry had fastened itself upon that trade union and was the power back of the organization.

Not only this, but it was connected with all of the travel of men who came to look upon the curiosities and wonders gathered here. People came thousands of miles just to see that temple, just to see that statue of the goddess, just to see the marvelous thing that could be witnessed in that theatre. Now, you see how deep-rooted this idolatry was. Their religion said, "I will give you a theater, I will give you a racecourse, I will give you festivals where you may drink out of every cup of pleasure, and where you may lie down on every bed of flowers, and where you may gratify every appetite of the body or of the mind, and I will give you gold that will glitter by day and by night, and I will give you everything that is beautiful to the eye and sweet to the taste and pleasant to the fancy, and thus I will make the perpetuity of this idolatry and the commercial prosperity of this city stand or fall together."

Such was the field to which Paul came. And how came he? Heard you any trumpet that announced his coming? Did any messenger go before him to say, "Lo, a king with his host cometh"? Had he letters of introduction to the bankers and priests and Asiarchs? He came afoot, walking in the dust. He came by himself. He came where the souls of these people were walled in by all of the power of this dark superstition, and walked up to the door and knocked, and he said, "Let me in with the gospel of Jesus Christ." And ignorance caught the knob of the door and said, "No." And demons roused up and put their shoulders against it and said, "No." And magic came and put its seal on the keyhole and said, "No." And commerce, in all of her mighty power, said "No." And games and festivals and amusements and howling mobs and roaring beasts in the arena came up and massed themselves against that door and said, "You cannot enter." But the text says, "I will tarry at Ephesus until Pentecost; for a great door and effectual is opened unto me, and there are many adversaries."

How, then, did he get it open? I paint a picture for you. John saw it in Apocalyptic vision on Patmos. I borrow the picture from the gallery of John, the great apostolic limner. He says, "I saw Jesus, exalted and glorified, and having at his girdle the keys of David with power to open and no man could shut, and with power to shut and no man could open." "This Jesus with the keys," says Paul, "will open that door for me." And the key is put in the lock, and the adversaries press themselves against the door, and the arm of Omnipotence opens it wide and crushes them that oppose. And Paul goes in with the power and the salvation of the gospel of Jesus Christ. The Lord pity the arrogant and vain and deceived and doomed man, though he be a preacher, that expects to go out and open the door of gospel acceptance against such adversaries as keep it shut, without reliance upon him who holds the keys of death and hell.

Listen to the Scriptures: The heart is locked. He opened Lydia's heart and Paul's gospel entered. Paul's tongue was locked and he opened him a door of utterance and breathed on him a divine afflatus, so that he spoke thoughts that breathed and words that burned. The Bible was locked and he opened the Scriptures and light after light flashed from heaven across its pages and made them luminous. Men were locked in unbelief and he opened unto them the door of faith and they saw the Son of God in his beauty. Enemies came and pressed upon God's people and hemmed them up, and he opened unto them a door of deliverance. Temptation shut them in and reached out in beguiling and seductive power to destroy them, and he opened a way of escape. Tyrants put them in prison, as Herod put Peter, and he opened the prison doors and let them out. Death came and put his cold seal on their dumb lips, and he opened the doors of death and called them back to life again. Hades shrouded their disembodied spirits and he opened the realm of Hades and called their spirits back again. Not only were the keys of death and hell at his girdle, but when heaven was shut, he opened that door and they entered in with singing and shouting and triumph.

Without such a door opener, what advantage have we in our perils and sufferings? 1 Corinthians 15:30-32: "And why stand we in jeopardy every hour? I protest by your rejoicing which I have in Christ Jesus our Lord, I die daily. If after the manner of men I have fought with beasts at Ephesus, what advantageth it me, if the dead rise not? let us eat and drink; for tomorrow we die." Why, there was a time there at Ephesus when they condemned him and they took him out to that theater and threw him to the lions and tigers, and it would seem they killed him and God raised him from the dead. I infer that from the passage in 2 Corinthians, where he said, "Brethren, I would not have you to be ignorant of the great trouble which came upon me in Asia, where my life was pressed out of measure, and the sentence of death was ended on me, but God delivered me from it and will deliver me from it again."

Let us consider another formidable adversary—the aroused and awful mob. Siberian wolves, in countless hordes, or such as followed Mazeppa, bound naked on the wild horse of the deserts—these with tireless speed and hungry eyes and cruel fangs and ominous howlings, are awful foes to a defenseless and belated traveler, but not so cruel and terrible as the Ephesian mob stirred to madness against Paul. Read their history in the downfall of Paris.

But how was this mob excited? Superstition, combining with self-interest, called the craftsmen's ring together. "Blow your trumpets and gather your workmen together and hold your secret conclave. Our craft is in danger. This man is ruining our trade. This image of Diana is brought into disrepute, whom all the world worshiped. He is turning upside down the prosperity of this city, and our harbors will not more have ships of trade and commerce, and the multitudes will no longer come unto our May festivals, and our city will parch like a desert spot if you do not stop this Paul. And if any man seeks to argue, drown his voice by continually howling: 'Great is Diana of the Ephesians!' "

And so the howling mob shut in around him, raging like the storm-tossed sea. And what said Paul? Into their fifty thousand glaring eyes of hate he looked and said, "I will tarry at Ephesus until Pentecost." The door of courage was opened unto him, sublime courage, the kind of courage that Luther had when he said, "I will go to the Diet at Worms, though there be as many devils there as there be tiles on the roof." "I will tarry here where God placed me, and I will rely upon the King of kings, who has the keys of death and hell, and finish my work," said Paul. He never left until that roar ceased.

Tradition says that one hundred thousand people were converted in that meeting. Go read the letter that Pliny wrote to the Roman emperor stating that the Christians had captured that part of the world, that they were everywhere, and that the altars of the gods were barren of gifts. Oh, it was a famous meeting, where men had religion enough to confess openly

their evil practices and forsake them and to burn, not sell
to others, the means of their unholy traffic.

Now, I will say this: If I have any religious conviction at
all; if I have any religion worth talking about; if I have
any definite or bright or sweet hope of heaven, it is all based
on just that uncompromising kind of preaching the gospel of
the Lord Jesus Christ. Whenever the church strikes hands of
friendship with the world, whenever it borrows the mantle of
idolatry, its power is gone. Whenever it makes alliance with
theaters, games, and infamous traffics, its power is gone. It
can cast out no devils, can break up no stronghold of the
enemy; it can only beguile—it cannot save. I would just say
this to the brethren: Where there is wealth and fashion and
amusement and gain, you have no power at all if you separate
from Jesus—none at all. Every vestige of your strength is
gone from you. You are like Samson shorn of his locks. You
must go out and stand with the Book in your hand that has
conquered every other book hitherto, and oppose it to all the
evil literature of the world, whether it comes in the guise of
philosophy or in the fairy garments of poetry, or in the rose-
colored costume of romance. The truth, the whole truth, and
nothing but the truth, as it comes from God—that is the sword
of the eternal Spirit by which alone we can win this fight.

We must just go to men, no matter how rich they are, no
matter how fashionable they are, no matter how deeply in-
trenched in custom and tradition their evil courses are—we
must go to them and say, "There is no compromise between
the religion of Jesus Christ and what you do. One must die.
We do not shake hands at all. We do not lie down in the
same bed. We do not rest under the shadow of the same
tree. We do not sing the same songs. We do not camp on
the same grounds. It is war, truceless war, that is never to
know an interval until victory or death comes to end the
contest." And given a little church, just a handful of brethren
and sisters who believe the Bible—I mean *believe* it—who believe what it says about death and hell and heaven and the

judgment; who believe that the Lord Jesus Christ, in omnipotent power, is with his people and standing right by them, having his presence with them, never stopping to ask which shall win and which shall not, but saying as he said to us, "Stand up and testify; he did not send us as philosophers; he sent us as witnesses to stand before the door of the heart and testify that the Lord Jesus Christ is the only hope of salvation. We bear witness to that fact. God did not put it upon us to go back and give any philosophical reasons for it at all. We come as witnesses to a fact, and a fact which has touched our own hearts and filled our own souls with peace that we hold up before you, and invite you in God's name to stand upon the same platform."

Given such a church, it will turn the world upside down. Do that and let alone apologies; quit putting your weak shoulder to the granite of God's revelation, as if without your prop it would turn over. You let it stand. It will stand. Do not defend it. Preach it! Bear witness to it, and rely upon him that sent you, and you will conquer.

Will you do that? Will this church do that? Will you promise? Will you covenant here today before God, that no matter how the city may increase in riches; no matter how many railroads may come; no matter how dark and pestilential a miasma of error may impregnate its atmosphere, and no matter if the vampires of evil from the depths of hell shall come and hover and brood over this city and darken it with outspread Plutonian pinions, will you, as a church, stand firm upon this, that there is no salvation except in repentance toward God and faith in the Lord Jesus Christ?

If you do, I can say this for you, that whatever other things may go down, whatever dynasties of kings may pass away and become a memory; whatever monuments of time, after becoming hoary with age, shall crumble in the dust and be swept away, or be buried under the accumulating sands of the ages, whatever revolutions may sweep over the earth, whatever stars may expire in darkness, your candlestick will

never be removed. It will be shining as a light in the darkness
when the trumpet sounds and the dead wake up to find the
Master come.

But when you forego it, now, or twenty, or a hundred or a
thousand years from now—when the simplicity of the gospel
is changed in your Sunday school teachings, in the lives of
our members, in its ordinances, in the purity and power of
its truth, God Almighty will remove the candlestick of this
church and there will be darkness where there had been a
bright, shining light. One of the sweetest thoughts that comes
to my mind is that when Jesus comes, the First Baptist Church
of Waco will be engaged in celebrating the Lord's Supper in
obedience to his commandment, "This do until I come," and
that from the communion table you will go to meet the Lord.